The Magnificent Showman

The Epic Films of Samuel Bronston

The Magnificent Showman

The Epic Films of Samuel Bronston

by Mel Martin

Published in the USA by:
BearManor Media
P O Box 71426
Albany, Georgia 31708
www.bearmanormedia.com

ISBN 978-1-59393-129-2

Printed in the United States of America.

Book & cover design by Darlene and Dan Swanson of Van-garde Imagery, Inc.

Contents

Introduction

It was 1961 and I was 13 years old. Sitting at my desk doing schoolwork, I turned on the radio station I always listened to when studying. Normally, I had rock 'n' roll on, but when I studied I always chose classical music because it was less distracting.

As the radio warmed up, some music was playing that caught my attention. I did not know what it was, but it was breathtaking. Transcendent. It took me to another place, another time. I remember waiting for the finish so the announcer would tell me what it was. My studying had come to a halt, as I stared at the radio.

The announcement never came. Instead, a commercial and then some more music followed. Dashing for the yellow pages, I looked up the radio station's telephone number, and finally talked to someone who knew what it was. "El Cid," he said. I asked what an "El Cid" was. A movie, they said, just opening in town.

The next day, I found the original soundtrack. The music was by Miklos Rozsa, and the illustration on the cover showed the film's title cut out of gigantic blocks of stone, with tiny pictures that illustrated scenes from the movie. Produced by Samuel Bronston, it said.

I played the album until I wore it out, especially because I kept playing the "Fight for Calahorra" track over and over. Moving the

stylus repeatedly to that track had inadvertently scratched the album. I vowed to buy another.

A few days later I saw the movie. Again, the magnificent music,
not coming out of a clock radio speaker, but grandly pouring forth
from a multi-channel first-run house sound system, now supple-
mented by sweeping, colorful vistas on a large screen, breathtaking camera work and an epic story, all combined once again to
take me to another place and time. It was magical.

How, I wondered, did this movie come to be? Who made it?
Was it a true story? Where was it filmed? How and where did they
get those thousands of people? That began the pursuit: more al-
bums by Rozsa, more movies to see over the next few years; *King of
Kings*, *55 Days at Peking*, *The Fall of the Roman Empire*.

Now Dimitri Tiomkin's music (*55 Days at Peking*, *The Fall of the
Roman Empire*, *Circus World*) was added to my growing shelf of vinyl.
Historical books on the Cid, the Fall of Rome, the Boxer Rebellion,
the paperback versions of the movie screenplays and, inevitably,
books on cinema.

As I began to learn about how movies were made, the hunger for
more knowledge about these historical movies began to grow, but
could not be satisfied. The old questions remained. Who was the
producer? I knew the name, of course, Samuel Bronston, but who
was he? How did thousands of extras, first-rate actors, and artisans
capable of creating the look of antiquity all meet on a flat plain
somewhere in Spain to recreate such thrilling motion pictures?

I waited in vain for the answers. In the sixties there were no
books that explained these epics, and, in particular, nothing substantial about Bronston and his collaborators.

Years later there were snippets; a few pages in Charlton Heston's books, articles on directors Anthony Mann and Nicholas
Ray. It was not enough. It never would be enough.

Hence, this book. It's a look at the Bronston epics, the rather amazing production details and the receptions the films had from critics and audiences. To talk about the films, one must talk about Samuel Bronston, from his youth, his early days in the film industry, his production of mega epics, his financial fall and the reasons behind it. In the course of this book we'll hear from Bronston's family, friends, and critics. We'll also hear from the people who helped make the films a reality.

Samuel Bronston was described by many over the years as a sort of Cecil B. DeMille character, and there is some truth to that. Bronston was driven to make "big" films. He obsessed over the details. No amount of money was too great so he could have accuracy in the sets and costumes. Bronston was not a director like DeMille, he was only a producer, yet he left a very personal imprint on all of his films. *King of Kings*, *El Cid*, and *The Fall of the Roman Empire*, in particular, are Bronston films, I think, more than Anthony Mann or Nicholas Ray films.

He was extremely creative, and brought new ideas for how films should be produced and distributed. His output of six major films in six years was unequaled by anyone else producing high quality epics. Having grown weary of the politics and mechanics of Hollywood, he created his own studios in Madrid, hiring some of the most respected and able directors, writers and designers available. That studio, with access to land and a large number of extras (including thousands from the Spanish Army), helped create a "factory" for epic films that was unmatched anywhere in the world. "Factory" might not be the best word, because it might imply shoddy or an assembly line. In point of fact, the production quality of the films was extremely high, and the Bronston films stand alone in sets, art direction and costuming.

Then, as quickly as Bronston's studios grew, it all collapsed as audiences' taste for epics vanished at the time *The Fall of the Roman Empire* was underway.

Bronston's operation sank in a flurry of lawsuits and fights with creditors, and over the rights to his films and their distribution.

It's clear there has been a decades long desire to see these films. The <u>DVD Newsletter</u> has ranked *El Cid* and *Fall of the Roman Empire*, *55 Days at Peking* and *Circus World* high on the list of titles movie fans want to see in DVD release. Now those prayers have been answered, with *El Cid* and *Fall of the Roman Empire* scheduled for release in early 2008 by the Weinstein Company. I was privileged to be interviewed for the *El Cid* DVD, and did the commentary on the *Fall of the Roman Empire* with Samuel Bronston's son, Bill. *55 Days at Peking* and *Circus World* are also scheduled to be released by the Weinstein Company in the coming months.

Certainly, this book is not everything there is to know, but my ardent hope is it will be a cool sip of knowledge for those who share the same thirst.

Foreword

Reading that my father was a "driven" man invariably makes me chuckle. The problem was he never learned to drive, and thus, was dependent on my mother to chauffer him everywhere – to and from the office – to appointments - and of course whenever they socially forayed out. In my child's view the most memorable of these forays were mysterious evening dress-up events. These night-time outings were invariably marked by my mother's full-length, perfume-imbued mink coat being thrown on the bed as a ritual signal just prior to their leaving. Of course as his business and career bloomed, the drive was handled by full time professionals and a progression of appropriate, "mogul" automobiles culminating in his Rolls in Madrid.

Naturally, the metaphor of being driven is deeply apt as Samuel Bronston was a man possessed all his life. He was possessed by an acute sense of his image first, an image that utterly ruled his internal life. "Samuel Bronston" was an icon to which Samuel Bronston swore eternal fealty. It was this former construct that mesmerized all his associates and potential investors to whom he predicted his unquestioned destiny to produce not just movies but phenomena that would transfigure all those vested in the sublime visions he held. From the very beginning, I believe his emancipation from the ignominy of being a poor refugee child, shuttled out of post revolutionary era Besarabia by an angst ridden pair of parents into the streets of Paris, hinged on creating a dazzling identity. In my father's psyche, there was no Samuel Bronston without the establishment of "Samuel Bronston". His was the lonely and shrewd task of fashioning, not only his movie project laden path forward, but the reputation of being impervious to failure, lack of funds, any doubts about his forgone imminent success, regardless of the specific situation in which he found himself.

Such metamorphosing early situations included; winning over my mother, who was the daughter of a solvent Russian expat businessman with an opulent movie theater and jewelry business in Paris, as his wife and early benefactor; handling his delicate and urgent emigration from France in 1937, then the journey through Belgium, London and immigrating to New York; meeting and persuading a US Congressman to help secure his naturalization and immediate relocation to Hollywood before he had barely kicked off the dust of Ellis Island; seeking to borrow a constant stream of money from a line of convinced backers that he would be – and was – a sure fire movie producer and engine for lucrative returns before ever having a studio minute to his credit; ingratiating himself under the nurture of BP Shulberg who entrusted my father to produce his first poignant black and white movies; surviving the catastrophic collapse of his simultaneous production aspirations with "A Walk in the Sun" and "Ten Little Indians".... and so it went, from frying pan to fire for his whole life. From peak to valley to peak, an unshakable conviction, a certitude, of his invincibility which became the magnet of his personality and ability to find backers, cash or endless credit to forge his professional life. His 'drive' was always in forward gear, pedal to the metal, with no rear view mirror, brakes, or critical insurance to cover liability losses at many points in his trip. In this journey, however, there were periods of desperate standstill, waiting, waiting for a breakthrough phone call. In this posture he spent vast time tortured and alone. This was the price for inventing his destiny and living by imagination, sheer will and the relentless hunt of bankable properties. But never, did he ever relinquish his sense of purpose or lack the infinite persuasive resources to captivate whomever he focused his attention and vision upon. Many of these amazing episodes are part of the story that Mel Martin spins here in this devoted biography.

This unique public identity to which my father was sworn in his deepest and personal heart of hearts was genuinely unforgiving. It kept him a psychological and business prisoner, and often, a fugitive from family intimacy, ordinary pleasures, personal peace, non-utilitarian friendships, and empathy with many of the closest relations around him who would often find themselves sequestered in his image castle. Critical to his self and public image was being an epic provider, first in name, second in largesse, which he delivered at great cost to all our day to day, in-depth, familiarity. He prided himself in the role of 'father' wherein his children were, like his cinematic productions, raised, managed and secured by teams of in-house caregivers. I think he had no internalized role model of intimacy and unconditional parental acceptance on which to draw, given his large family, beleaguered parents, ripped by the economic and political tumult that buffeted his formative first 25 years.   From what were real or experienced insecurities and indelible perceptions of early poverty, and lack of work norms, he constructed architectural girders to counteract and hide whatever he disdained as ordinary. His designs from the start till the end were extraordinary and epic. He fought to breathe opulence, status and independent expression.

The Samuel Bronston I knew lived at the behest of his "Samuel Bronston". From the former, a Russian Jew, the third child of nine, multi-lingual, multi-national, shy, easily awed, deeply appreciative of people's kindness, patient, gregarious. From this alloy came the river of intuition, love and regard that drew him to his movie subjects and drew people to his calling. This was the most attractive, polite, charismatic human being that walked the earth. Both Samuel and "Samuel" were the epitome of gentlemanliness. His impeccable suited appearance every day of his life, gracious and suave demeanor, utterly infectious, deep chuckling laugh which came easily and often, the sentimental tears that fell with equal frequency, his overwhelming sweetness and charm, were a phenomenon to witness and experience first hand. Dad had very large blue eyes whose penetration and sparkle were formidable. He exuded confidence and style without arrogance or domination. He was an ultimate tasteful showman in his trade, second to none.

Uncomfortable reading, he experienced stories read to him with a possessive passion, swept up in epic heroes, heroism, family integrity, boundary less romance and historic grandeur. There was never a time I remember when he was not cradling a book title into which his compulsion to "produce" was not all consuming. "Can you imagine", he would finally say, "We'll announce the next Samuel Bronston Production of . . . " Story properties were deliciously his. as long as the chance of becoming a financed project existed. Unlike oil well exploration where a dry hole ends the drill, potential story properties have much less clear endpoints before they must be abandoned. These literary love affairs became a living and major subtext and foster member of our family's circle.

The "Samuel Bronston" was a supreme opportunist, an instinct built into the epicenter of his earliest and life long machinery. A self-styled Rooseveltian Democrat, "Bronston" was comfortable marketing his projects to, and exploiting support from, Republicans, aristocrats, fascists, papal Catholics, dictators, any banker or potential lender alive if it meant keeping on his "Drive". He was anything but an ideologue, or for that matter did he remotely identify with Hollywood's corporate orthodoxy. Ironically, the absence of either of these adaptive frameworks, left him with a strategic, operational ambiguity that resulted in his ultimate complete business crash. On the one hand was his unbridled conviction to innovate, at a breathtaking level, in all aspects of the industry and, on the other, having no tried and true objective administrative modus operandi to set personnel performance and accountability measures to secure his gains.

The Samuel Bronston Production company mix he assembled in Spain, contained literary, artisan and design genius that had never been rivaled. "Samuel" surrounded himself with tiers of associates towards whom he exercised an unshakable bond who many times over squandered and betrayed his trust and generosity. Around him collected many carnivores, I guess that goes with the business, but was hugely intensified by my father's uncritical emotional support. During the years in Spain, a key cadre of company execs and those sensitively placed in the studio reaped immense personal fortunes from the kings ransom of goods, currency, and political influence. Yet, for both Samuels, family and public honor was inviolable and his loyalty profound notwithstanding the resultant commercial suicide. When, at the end, "Samuel Bronston" fell to earth in ashes, the remaining Samuel Bronston rusted out into the cruel labyrinth of his slowly encroaching Alzheimer's demise.

As the reader ponders this book, and hopefully revisits the riveting complexity, elegance and drama of the movies of "Samuel Bronston", I encourage you to also seek access to the inchoate soul of Samuel Bronston, who, maybe like the Wizard of Oz with all his foibles and happenstances, architected the daunting light and sound show to impress and speak to all his adopted society. The effort truly embodies an intention of enhancing quality of life whether ethically and historically considered or hopelessly, romantically misfabricated. The journey, the chauffeured drive, is definitely compelling and inspiring.

Bill Bronston M.D.
Carmichael California

Preface
Why the Bronston Films? Why Now?

Alfred Hitchcock when dealing with an actress who was over intellectualizing the process of preparing for a role told her, "It's only a movie." So it is with the films of Samuel Bronston, but what movies they were!

Unlike other films, epics are in a world of their own. An epic can be described as the struggle of great men and women to create ideas and movements bigger than themselves; ideas that move a large group of people or civilization forward to some higher goal. Through the camera of the filmmakers, we see places we could not go, things we could not experience; we are eyewitnesses to great events or ideas that hopefully inspire us.

Many of Bronston's films have similar themes; sweeping changes are taking place while heroes hold on to their integrity and a physical place. It is central to *El Cid, The Fall of the Roman Empire*, and *55 Days at Peking*. It is visible in *John Paul Jones* and *King of Kings*. It is perhaps the essence of the epic, and it was important in other films of the period that Bronston did not produce like *The Alamo, Ben-Hur* and *Khartoum*. Also very visible in the Bronston films is a sense of pan-nationalism: Many people from many countries or creeds coming together for some higher purpose.

These larger themes differentiate the epic from the rest of cinema. These same themes are found in all the Bronston epics, which could well serve as archetypes of the genre. These films are not bubbly romances, or cops, bullets and car chases; they are about humans stretched to the limits against societal forces that bring change that could be good or evil. They are about standing one's ground in the face of incalculable odds.

The odds were against the Bronston films as well. To get them made, Bronston had to devise new ways to finance and distribute them.

Spain was a country that had no oil of its own. Through the force of his personality he convinced the DuPonts to let him broker oil into Spain. The DuPonts didn't want Spanish pesetas, which could not be taken out of the country, so Bronston took the pesetas to finance his films, giving money from the films' profits back to DuPont in dollars. Soon, Bronston was serving as middleman in many different forms of commodities trading. It was a wholly unique method of financing films. Bronston also received investments from businessmen not connected with Hollywood. He uniquely sold distributorships nation by nation, and populated his casts with actors and actresses from many countries so his motion pictures would have appeal in each country.

Bronston was driven by his own muse to build sets on a scale never before accomplished. They were filled with detail and historical accuracy. No expense was too great to Bronston if it was in the service of the story. As people would hear him say over and over, "Money is no object."

He lived a life of contradictions. Bronston was a Jew who had the ear of the Pope. He believed in heroes and leaders, yet made films under a fascist dictatorship in Spain. He was a strong believer in America and American ideals of freedom, yet hired writers who had been blacklisted and forced into a new life in Europe. He wanted to make big Hollywood films, but his ideas were discarded by the film community so he built his own Spanish "Hollywood" and made his epic productions the way he wanted to without traditional financing.

He assembled an enviable collection of top-ranking directors, actors and technicians who shared his uncommon goal to make epic films with style and substance that spoke to cinemagoers in a visual and artistic language that was unique.

Bronston did not make the first epics, or the last. But he was the last to make them in his particular way, with attention to detail that was simply too expensive for others to emulate. Indeed, as we will see as the story unfolds, it was too expensive for Bronston as well.

These films could be remade today, but never duplicated. Computer graphics would substitute for Bronston's expansive sets, and computer generated armies would substitute for the thousands of extras that donned Bronston-produced costumes.

In fact, after decades of epics being absent from the cinema, recent years have seen a revival. Films like *Gladiator, Alexander, Troy* and *Days of Heaven* have been produced in the last few years. While these films have tried to recapture the "feel" of the sixties epics, they are somewhat arid and cold. *Gladiator* was a successful revenge movie (and a virtual remake of Bronston's *The Fall of the Roman Empire*), *Alexander, Troy* and *Days of Heaven* had beautiful production designs but were generally found wanting by critics and audiences. The computer work of rendering sets and armies was obvious, and not totally fulfilling. As we view them, our mind keeps saying the scene is fake, and while we are deconstructing the special effects, we are drawn away from the movie itself.

After *El Cid*, the Bronston films had weaknesses too. They were often financially troubled productions, a result of Bronston trying to do bigger and bigger pictures that outran the money coming in from the previous efforts. The later films were weaker on character, sometimes leaning on the spectacular while submerging the subtle. The overall effect, however, was memorable. One couldn't help but be awed by the lovingly created details of sets and costumes, of photography and music. Epics only succeed if you believe what you are seeing on the screen, and the Bronston films looked as "believable" as any films ever made.

Film audiences tired of the sixties epics, probably brought on by the fatigue from films like *Cleopatra*. There were simply too many of these films. The success of the big epics like *Ben-Hur* brought many lesser films, followed by dozens of cheap Hercules and Samson films that were shot on a production line in Italy. There were perhaps too many royal entrances to ancient cities; too many chariot races and sword fights.

The empire that Bronston created got caught between making the kinds of quality films he wanted to make and a public that had tired of films with these spectacular themes.

Always the showman, Bronston tried to adjust, recalibrating his goals with smaller films like *Circus World* (1964) and future productions like *Brave New World*. He still wanted to make epics, and announced pre-production activities on *Isabella of Spain* with Glenda Jackson, *Captain Kidd, Knight of La Mancha,* and *Nightrunners of Bengal* and others, but in the end it was not to be. The unconventional financing, the cost-no-object sets and costumes, were destined to be artifacts of a kind of moviemaking we would never see again.

Through it all, Bronston was Bronston: big films, big ideas. He was one of a kind. Nothing much has been written about Bronston, and that is both sad and a missed opportunity. He opened

Spain to the movie industry, and it flourishes there still today. He opened filmgoers' minds to spectacular widescreen vistas and a glorious past that we could not have experienced without him.

This volume remembers the movies and the man behind them. We remember him for his vision, so much of it achieved, and for his failures, as time and money ran out. We remember him for taking us places we could not go, and showing us things we would otherwise never see.

Samuel Bronston has been gone for more than a dozen years; his last film was made more than 40 years ago. It is time to remember Samuel Bronston, who dreamed important dreams and made them live and breathe on the big screen and in our memories.

One aside: No book, however ambitious, can capture everything about a man and his work. Many of Bronston's closest associates are dead; many of the actors are gone, as are all of the directors of the Bronston films. The author has relied on interviews with writers, associates, family members and studio production details to stitch together this portrait of the Bronston films and Bronston himself. Memories fade, and are sometimes revised. The author has done his best to sort fact from fiction and tell the story of a man whose impact on the film industry and the art was far reaching and whose films continue to inspire and entertain.

Acknowledgements

No book comes to life from just the author alone. In exploring the colorful life of Samuel Bronston I had a lot of help along the way, and want to thank the many people who showed me many courtesies and took time out to reflect on the memories of Bronston during the incredible years when he was a true force in the creation of memorable motion pictures.

First, and foremost, I'd like to thank Dr. William Bronston, who shared stories about his dad, insights into his personality, and spent many hours with me going through papers and photos from his dad's career. This book simply would not have been possible without his comments and criticisms.

I'd also like to thank Norma Barzman, a terrific author on her own, who graciously told me the stories about her late husband Ben who was the principal writer for the incredible scripts of *El Cid* and *The Fall of the Roman Empire*. Her memories added much needed depth to the text, and illuminated the stories about how those films came to be. Her own book, *The Red and the Blacklist*, details her life with Ben and what it was like being expatriates and living their lives in Spain.

Bernard Gordon also contributed to this story. Gordon worked for Bronson on *El Cid, 55 Days at Peking* and *Circus World*. He wrote those films while weighed down with the stigma, like Barzman, of being a victim of the Hollywood blacklist. He was very helpful when I visited him in Hollywood, and he has vivid memories of his work on the Bronston pictures. Sadly, Bernard Gordon died in May, 2007 at age 88. I will always appreciate his kindness to me and his contributions to many of the films he made better throughout his long and productive career.

The author is also indebted to Peter Besas in Madrid, author of *Behind the Spanish Lens*, a first-rate book about how Spain became a major production hub in the 1960s and '70s. He was most helpful in describing how Bronston fit into the Spanish production scene, and he was most kind sharing his memories of his meeting with Bronston as Bronston's empire began to fade.

It was a thrill to talk to Ray Bradbury, and hear his stories about writing for *King of Kings*. His prologue and narration for the film are some of the best written words in all the Bronston films.

Special thanks also go to Sheldon Hall in England, who has written and researched the Bronston films extensively, and kindly provided European trade papers from the period that helped me trace Bronston's comings and goings.

I also owe thanks to the attorneys who were involved in the Bronston bankruptcy and his subsequent charges of perjury. Walter Phillips Jr. was an Assistant United States Attorney and led the government's perjury case against Bronston. Sheldon Elsen defended Bronston in that case, and in other civil actions that flowed from Bronston's financial problems. Both men were helpful in filling in details of the period, and provided their own perceptions about Bronston's plight.

I'm also anxious to thank Dorothea Bronston, now living in London, for the time she spent talking with me about her life with

Sam during the production of the epic films. She was most helpful in illuminating what the wife of a movie producer was like during the time Bronston was at his most productive in Madrid.

Closer to home I'd like to thank broadcaster extraordinaire Dick Warsinske for reading the book's chapters as they were produced and providing helpful hints and criticisms.

Thanks also to Ben Ohmart of BearManor Media for taking the book on and believing in the subject matter.

Finally, a big thank you to my wife and companion, Joan, who encouraged me to finally write this book and gave many ideas for improvement.

Mistakes in the book are mine and mine alone. Inspiration for the book came from those listed above and many others unnamed who were so generous with their time and thoughts.

John Paul Jones (1959)

*"The Man and the Battle Cry that
Shaped American Naval History."*

Director: John Farrow, **Writers**: John Farrow, Ben Hecht (uncredited), Jesse Lasky Jr. and Clements Ripley. **Producer**: Samuel Bronston; **Cast**: Robert Stack, Bette Davis, Marisa Pavan, Charles Coburn and Macdonald Carey; **Released**: Warner Brothers; Shot in Technirama (aspect Ratio 2.35:1); **Running time**: 126 minutes.

*J*ohn Paul Jones is notable as the first epic film produced by Samuel Bronston, and the first film he shot in Spain. Samuel Bronston had the idea of a John Paul Jones movie going back to 1946. As he studied U.S. history preparing for his citizenship test, the story of John Paul Jones resonated with him, and he kept it in the back of his mind.

At the time of production, Bronston was quoted as saying, "For a dozen years I tried to make this picture in Hollywood. Several major studios tried too, but the heavy budget necessary to make it scared them off and made it impossible for me to secure the financial support I needed. There were many in Hollywood who said that *John Paul Jones* was a picture that could never be made.

"It probably never would have been made if I hadn't succeeded in setting it up on a 5-million-dollar budget by filming it on locations with the help of private money. There's not one dollar of movie money in our company. Our backers are men who believe in the project. "

This was an early indication of Bronston's disdain for Hollywood and the difficulties he faced trying to make quality films under the weight of what he saw as timid studios and endless bureaucracy. He was proud the film had no "movie money" in it. He was free to make the kinds of films he wanted to make, depending on the studios only for distribution.

The film earned only one million dollars in domestic release. Warner Brothers purchased the rights to the film, but was unhappy with its eventual performance, and Warners sold the rights back to Bronston for a re-release, but the film did no better a second time.

Bill Bronston says the film finally came into being at the urging of Admiral Chester Nimitz, a naval war hero who had been introduced to Bronston.

"My dad was really a wheeler dealer, and he made great inroads into the Navy. You know, the political part of the Navy, not the military part but rather the high end part, and he somehow became friends with Chester Nimitz. This was already after the war and Nimitz was this old, incredible retired, sort of Pope of the Navy, and this great hero. And my dad tells me that Nimitz literally took him to Spain, introduced him to Franco, and settled him in Spain to make *John Paul Jones* because the Navy needed a movie to emulate its history. And there had never been a movie made about the American Revolution to that time.

"He got financing, partly from the Navy, a lot of support from the Navy – because when you look at the credits at the end of the movie it's all from the Navy Department and he was constantly trafficking with these naval bureaucrats to make the movie. In the process of establishing himself in that movie he somehow gained the unconditional support of the Franco regime, up and down.

"I went there in the summer while they were shooting that movie, which was the only movie ever that I was actually on the set of while they were shooting, in my whole life. I was there for a month in Alicante while they were shooting, and I took a boyfriend of mine, a fraternity brother, and we went to Europe in the middle of my sophomore year in college, which had to be '58. My dad was in Madrid running the operation from there. He was out of sight, out of mind. We talked on the phone but I was in the South, on location, going out every day on these galleons, on these boats, in order to shoot stills for the movie with a Leica that he had bought me when he and I flew together to come to Europe."

The film was influenced by the Cold War that was at its height in the late fifties. Bronston said at the time he wanted a film about what made America great.

"Democratic. That's the word for this picture. Five governments – America, England, France, Italy and Spain – are giving me a lot of co-operation, too."

The irony was that Spain was hardly a democracy, but with Franco's help, Bronston could get things done, red tape cut, and mount a major motion picture for a fraction of the cost of doing his tribute to the U.S. Navy in the United States.

Another important point was that *John Paul Jones* marked the first time Bronston had financing from the DuPont family, specifically Pierre DuPont III. The DuPonts were always looking for patriotic enterprises, and this film measured up. It was good for everyone. Bronston got guarantees of financing from the DuPonts, while the DuPonts could participate in something that had patriotism, morality and spectacle. DuPont was able to work with Bronston to create a complicated financial arrangement where DuPont could pay expenses with Spanish pesetas which could not be taken out of the country. The DuPont relationship crumbled into acrimony as you will read later, and the enmity between Bronston and the DuPonts, coupled with extravagant budgets and loss of interest in spectacular films by the public, would lead to the total destruction of the Bronston empire.

The Film

The film begins in the present day (1959) on the deck of a U.S. Battleship while the commander lectures his men while Max Steiner's score echoes the strains of "Yankee Doodle" in the background. John Paul Jones (played by Robert Stack) is held up as an example of greatness to the young sailors, and identified as the first man to sail the American flag into foreign waters. The commander goes on to say, "It was he, more than anyone else, who set the pattern of everything about us."

Then the movie changes gears for a flashback to 1759, and moves to Scotland showing the young Jones making fun of British soldiers, who are harassing Scotsmen because they were wearing kilts.

The young Jones is interested in the sea, and as a very young man of 14 signs on as a ship's boy.

As the movie progresses, it is now a few years before the Declaration of Independence, and John Paul is now an owner of a ship and proprietor of a thriving business in the West Indies.

In the film, Jones kills a mutinous sailor and goes ashore to report what had happened to the authorities. He is told by the British Magistrate to leave as soon as possible, and not wait for a court trial sitting in jail, perhaps for years.

Jones leaves, taking the name John Paul Jones so he won't be known and leaves for America. He chooses Fredericksburg, Virginia to settle, because it is where his brother lives, but upon arriving Jones learns his brother has died, so Jones inherits the family farm, and settles in with the idea of living off the land as a well-to-do member of the gentry.

At this point in the film, Patrick Henry (played by Macdonald Carey) appears. Jones hires Henry as his lawyer, and Henry invites Jones to a party. Not happy with the manners of some British soldiers, Jones strikes one knocking him down. The incident plants the seeds of Jones resentment of the British.

He also meets and falls in love with Dorothea Dandridge (played by Erin O'Brien).

He tires of farming, and loses his love to Patrick Henry, and is now in the middle of the American Revolution.

Jones accepts a commission as the second in command of a Naval Ship in the fledgling United States Navy; formed as an answer to the famed and formidable British Navy that threatens the Revolution.

Jones demonstrates that he is a capable sailor and leader of men, and gets the honor of raising the first American flag. Without firing a shot, Jones and his marines take over a British fort in the West Indies, capturing gunpowder for the budding revolution.

Jones continues to plunder the British, and as America signs the Declaration of Independence, Jones gets a command of his own on the Providence. Jones learns his family farm has been burned by the British, further hardening his views on the War.

Despite Jones effectiveness and heroism, he is put at the bottom of the command list, and angrily heads to Valley Forge to confront General Washington and threaten to leave the Navy.

Finding Washington desperate, facing the prospect of a decimated and frostbitten Army, Jones is inspired by Washington's patriotism and agrees to go back to sea regardless of the rank he is given.

Washington suggests Jones fit out the *Ranger*, and break the British blockade and get to France to tell Benjamin Franklin that the country is in dire shape and that more soldiers are needed.

Jones does just that, and while meeting with Franklin he also happens upon his new love interest, Aimee de Tellison, played by Marisa Pavan.

Jones now has a plan to attack the British at Whitehaven, and burn ships, attack the cannons at the fort, and steal ammunition to help the Revolution.

Jones runs into politics and delays, and asks the French for a new ship as the *Ranger* has been recalled to America. A Dutch ship is purchased, and christened the *Bon Homme Richard*, named in honor of Franklin's *Poor Richard's Almanac*.

Jones attacks the British *HMS Serapis*, and is victorious but loses his ship after ramming the enemy and commandeers the *Serapis*. During the pitched battle, Jones utters his famous "I have not yet begun to fight" cry.

Jones is called back to America where he argues persuasively for a professional Navy before the Marine Commission. He wants to see well-equipped ships, and highly trained officers, but his suggestions are financially out of reach of the new country.

Bitter and disappointed, Jones offers his services to Russia, and meets with Catherine the Great (played by Bette Davis). He wins many battles for the Russians, against great odds. But Jones has become very sick and is slowly dying. He returns to France, where he is being taken care of by Franklin, and Aimee.

While in bed, Jones dictates the Navy code, and the scene dissolves to shots of our modern Navy while Jones voice can be heard: "The keel timber of this new Navy must be in the selection of the list of officers. It is by no means enough an officer be a capable mariner. He must be that, of course. But he must also be a great deal more. He must, as well, be a gentleman of liberal education, with a fine manner, punctilious courtesy and the nicest sense of personal honor. He should be the soul of tact, patience, firmness, justice and charity. As he should be universal in his rewards, so should he be judicial in reproof. When a commander has properly exercised these qualities, he has only to await the appearance of the enemy. His ship and his men will be ready."

The History

Much of the movie was based on a Samuel Elliot Morrison's biography of the naval hero that was published the year the film was released.

History was not courteous enough to exactly follow the plot laid down by Farrow and his writers. In reality, John Paul Jones was involved in the slave trade, but later felt it was immoral. The film has him come to this decision much earlier. John Paul Jones was a better commander than a politician, and the screenplay hints at this, but does not show much that is decisive in understanding Jones' character. In history, Jones visited his brother's plantation more than once, and, in fact, it was his brother, not a magistrate, who suggested John Paul change his name to John Paul Jones. As far as is known, Jones never knew Patrick Henry, but their friendship allows for major plot points in the film. The Battle of Jones against the *HMS Serapis* was pretty accurate for a feature film and exciting with cannons blasting and a heroic Max Steiner score. Jones, who was basically unemployed after the war, did in fact go to Russia and enter into the employ of Catherine the Great. Unlike the movie version, where he is cared for by Benjamin Franklin, Jones instead died alone in Paris in a third-floor apartment. He was buried in Paris, but in 1905 his remains were brought to the United States and he was re-buried at the United States Naval

Academy in Annapolis. The funeral oration was done by Theodore Roosevelt.

The Production

The film was really the first major production by Bronston that was largely done abroad. There were location shots at St. James Palace in London, in Colonial Williamsburg in Virginia, in Versailles, and in Madrid. Most of the naval battles were fought near Denia in Spain. Denia was chosen for its attractive small harbor, which is halfway between Valencia and Alicante on the Mediterranean.

Bronston was able to secure the Royal Palace in Madrid. It was redressed, and the throne room became the throne room for Catherine the Great with the addition of a few banners bearing the Imperial Russian seal.

In many ways, the "stars" of the film are the ships that carried the cast and crew and participated in the dramatic recreations of the famous naval battles that *John Paul Jones* depicts. Bronston invested $300,000 in the ships, and workers spent two years getting the ships ready. The two largest ships, the *Bonhomme Richard* and the *Serapis* were full scale replicas, and at the time of the filming were the only deep water ships of their kind to be used in the production of the movie. The hulls were located by Allen Villiers, who had skippered the *Mayflower II* on its historic Atlantic crossing. Villiers was one of the great authorities on sailing ships, and Bronston hired him as a technical advisor, and to supervise the construction and refitting of ships as the major props on the movie. Villiers remembered seeing the hulls of the two ships in Sicily, so they were located and towed to Ostia in Italy to begin their transformation from brigantines into fully rigged frigates. Once they had been built up and matched to plans of the original ships, Villiers sailed them the 800 miles to Denia on the Eastern coast of Spain. A third ship used in the film was the *Concepcion Masiques*. The Spanish Schooner was located in Barcelona, where it had been used for hauling fruit and salt. Bronston leased it, then had it converted into a two-masted frigate. It performed double duty in the film, first playing *The Betsy*, Jones' first ship, and later as *The Providence*, which took Jones to Europe.

As in his later films, there were touches of detail that spoke to the volumes of research done in pre-production. For example, in the original script Jones is referred to as "Admiral" by members of Catherine the Great's court in Russia. But later research showed that Jones would have been more properly referred to as "Excellency," so the script was changed.

Even in this early film, Bronston was the consummate hustler. Robert Stack, in his autobiography *Straight Shooting*, has an illuminating incident from the production.

"Sam had discovered that many large corporations had enormous assets in Spain which were frozen unless they were reinvested locally. Pierre DuPont, under Sam's influence, agreed to put up five million dollars in frozen funds to produce our movie. Sam's financial manipulations rivaled those of an international diplomat. He raised huge sums of money as if by magic. His wheeler-dealer ways with cash extended to the cast and crew. One day he showed up on the set with an enormous carpetbag full of exotic currencies – pfennigs, pesetas, francs, lira and a variety of others I had never seen before, announcing that the currency represented my week's salary. 'I don't know what this stuff is,' I said. 'It could be Confederate money. Give me something I can spend in the good ole US of A.' Bronston was never at a loss for words. In the course of the shooting, he managed to run up an enormous tab at the local bar. Instead of cash, he closed out his accounts with the Spanish bartender by inviting them to the set to watch the filming. But in spite of it all, I liked old Sam - he did give me the part!"

The Cast

Bronston showed an amazing ability to put together a first-class cast for *John Paul Jones*, something he would repeat in all his later productions. The lead, Robert Stack, was an odd choice to play Jones. He was much taller than the historical character, and had been in Hollywood for almost 20 years as an actor, most notably at the time playing Elliot Ness in *The Untouchables* on TV.

Stack was born in Los Angeles in 1919, but his parents divorced when Robert was one years old, and his mother took him to Europe. He learned to speak French and Italian, but did not become fluent in English until after his return to the States when he was six. He was considered a bit of a loner as he grew up, and did not play team sports but was an excellent skeet shooter.

He majored in drama at USC, and fell under contract at Universal in 1939. He co-starred with Deanna Durbin in *First Love*, his debut film. Stack played in a variety of films, including Westerns, war movies and adventures, and starred in the first commercial 3-D movie, *Bwana Devil*, with Barbara Britton and Nigel Bruce in 1952. After the four-year run of *The Untouchables*, he continued to work steadily, and seemed most comfortable doing a parody of his straight-laced character in a series of comedies, including *Caddyshack II, 1941* and *Airplane!* Stack hosted the popular TV program *Unsolved Mysteries* for almost 15 years. He died of a heart attack in 2003.

Bette Davis, cast as Catherine the Great, was another unlikely actress for the film. Davis was born 1908 in Massachusetts. She attended numerous acting academies and made her Broadway debut in 1923 in *Broken Dishes*. By 1930 she had been hired by Universal Pictures, appearing in *The Bad Sister* in 1931, but her career appeared to be heading nowhere.

In 1932, she was signed to a multi-year deal by Warner Brothers, and received good notices for her role in *The Man Who Played God*, starring George Arliss. She impressed again in *Of Human Bondage* (1934) and went on to receive best actress Oscars for *Dangerous* (1935) and *Jezebel* (1938). She was Warner Bros.' leading actress of the forties, but by the end of the decade her career began to trail off. It picked up again when she received an Oscar nomination for her role in *All About Eve* (1950). She came to public attention again, playing an insane child star, in Robert Aldrich's *What Ever Happened to Baby Jane?* (1962). Davis, a 10-time Oscar nominee, is still considered one of the greatest actresses in film history. Davis died of breast cancer in 1989 in France.

Marisa Pavan, who played John Paul Jones' love interest in the film, has had a varied career in films and television. Born in Italy in 1932, she is the twin sister of actress Pier Angeli. She came to the United States in 1950 and was Oscar nominated for best supporting actress in *The Rose Tattoo* (1955). Other films include *Solomon and Sheba, The Man in the Gray Flannel Suit*, and television parts in *Playhouse 90, The F.B.I., The Rockford Files, McMillan & Wife* and *Wonder Woman*.

Charles Coburn, who played Benjamin Franklin, was born in Georgia in 1877. He appeared on Broadway many times, and came to Hollywood in the late 1930s. Notable film performances were in *Edison, the Man, The Story of Alexander Graham Bell, The Devil and Miss Jones, Kings Row*, Hitchcock's *The Paradine Case*, and several TV performances, including *The Bob Cummings Show, General Electric Theater, The Betty White Show,* and *Kraft Television Theater*. He won an Oscar as best supporting actor in 1944 for *The More the Merrier*. He was the grandfather of actor James Coburn. Coburn died in 1961 in New York City of heart failure.

Playing Patrick Henry was Macdonald Carey. Perhaps best known today to soap opera fans for playing Dr. Tom Horton on NBC's *Day of Our Lives* for thirty years, Carey had an active film career before he ever came to television. He was born in Iowa in 1913 and made his debut in the 1942 comedy, *Take a Letter, Darling*. One of his most well-known roles was in Alfred Hitchcock's *Shadow of a Doubt* (1943). The film was one of Hitchcock's favorite films, and starred Joseph Cotten. Other notable film roles for Carey included *Wake Island, Streets of Laredo, Comanche Territory*, and *The Great Missouri Raid* (as Jesse James). In the sixties, he had moved almost completely to television, appearing on *Alfred Hitchcock Presents, The Outer Limits, Burke's Law, Branded, Run for Your Life* and *Ben Casey*. Carey died in 1994 of lung cancer.

One member of the cast few people would notice was Bronston's wife, Dorothea. She told me Sam didn't approve, but the director was desperate for women in a big scene with Bette Davis.

"And John Farrow wanted me to take a part in the film. I'm not an actress and he waited until Sam went out of town and [Farrow] said, 'I want you in the film.' I said, 'Well, I can't take any special part in that film. Sam doesn't want me to act.' So he had collected as many of the American women that he could in that film, and they were playing the roles of ladies in Bette Davis' court. Anyway, so I got the lady-in-waiting next to Bette Davis. I liked her, actually. I like anybody that has spunk and doesn't get pushed around and is intelligent and is a good actress."

The Critics

The film did not do well at the box office or with the critics.

Variety said, "*John Paul Jones* has some spectacular sea action scenes and achieves some freshness in dealing with the Revolutionary War. But the Samuel Bronston production doesn't get much firepower into its characters. They end, as they begin, as historical personages rather than human beings."

"John Farrow's direction of such scenes as the battle of Jones' *Bon Homme Richard* with the British *Serapis* is fine, colorful and exciting. Perhaps because Jones himself was a man of action, the story gets stiff and awkward when it moves off the quarterdeck and into the drawing room."

Bosley Crowther of the *New York Times* was not much kinder: "For, once more, the talents and resources of a lot of people and a large studio, John Farrow, writer-director, and a considerable cast of minor stars have been put to the tiresome task of shaping a flow of ponderous pictorial tableaus through which a solemn masculine figure, more myth than man, parades. The father of American sea power and the naval hero of the Revolutionary War is given no more depth or salty flavor than a costumed dummy in the window of a department store.

"As for portly Bette Davis, she is called upon to play Russia's Catherine the Great as though she was more interested in having Jones as a fast lover than as the post-Revolution admiral of her fleet. This is a dismal comedown for a star who once played good historical roles.

"All in all, this is an unexciting picture, so far as dramatic action is concerned, and utterly unexpressive of the recorded nature and character of John Paul Jones."

The film wasn't even a hit in the Bronston family. Dorothea Bronston, now living in London, told me it was far from her favorite of her husband's films.

"Well, I wasn't allowed to dislike anything, actually. Sam said once, if the baby is born then so be it, it's yours, you don't talk badly about it. But now it doesn't make any difference. I couldn't stand the music that went on in *John Paul Jones*, and I thought that Robert Stack was very wooden. It was the first film that he made when I was with him [Bronston] and I can remember I was struck dumb, actually, and I wasn't used to expressing myself under those circumstances. So I was in the motion picture theater – it was just a screening for some important people – and when we came out everybody said, 'Well, what did you think of this film? Wasn't it wonderful?' And all I wanted to do was get out of there so I could collect myself because I didn't think the film was very good at all.

"It was certainly miscast. Actually, I'll tell you something interesting. James Cagney was the one that Sam wanted for that. And Cagney would have been interested in doing it but his brother was an agent or something for Jimmy so he didn't think this was going to be any good so he warned him against it. And he didn't do it and it wasn't any good, actually, I don't think."

Summing Up

John Paul Jones was a "big" film, and the beginning of the Bronston epic period. As his first major endeavor on his own, it contained many of the themes that would sustain the other Bronston epics, the creation or decline of a nation (*El Cid, The Fall of the Roman Empire*) and a hero who was troubled yet triumphant by summoning his own skills against great odds (*El Cid, King of Kings, 55 Days at Peking, Circus World*)

The acting was generally weak, the camera work was not inspired, but clearly Bronston was determined to make a name for himself.

The film has some good action scenes, and Bronston could never have mounted a production like this in Hollywood. As many filmmakers learned later, production on the water is not easily done, and often can result in disaster and massive cost over-runs.

With *John Paul Jones,* Bronston had set in place his skills at managing a large and complicated enterprise, showed he could snap up first-class talent in terms of a name cast, and could bring to the screen a large scale historical drama that was uplifting and could be aimed at an international audience.

In context, *John Paul Jones* was just baby steps, but it was only the beginning. The great films were yet to come, but the outlines of the Bronston moviemaking apparatus could be seen taking form.

King of Kings

"A story of the Christ — The Glory
of His spoken words."

Released: 1961; **Producer**: Samuel Bronston, Alan Brown, Jaime Prades; **Director**: Nicholas Ray; Screenplay: Philip Yordan; Cinematography: Manuel Berenguer, Milton R. Krasner, Franz Planer; **Film Editing**: Harold F. Kress, Renee Lichtig; **Art Direction**: Enrique Alarcon; **Music**: Miklos Rozsa; **Cast**: Jeffrey Hunter, Siobhan McKenna, Hurd Hatfield, Ron Randell, Viveca Lindfors, Rita Gam, Carmen Sevilla; **Released**: MGM; **Running time**: 161 minutes; shot in Super Technirama 70 (Aspect Ratio 2.20:1)

King of Kings was a big film for the Bronston organization. Bronston wanted to remake the silent 1927 DeMille film of the life of Christ, and he had no doubts he could create a reverent box office smash. Budgeted at eight million dollars, it took in three times that amount. It started strongly at the box office, comparing favorably with *Ben-Hur's* opening, but eventually receipts tapered off and while profitable, it was not the tremendous hit Bronston had hoped for.

In some ways, it was ironic for Bronston to take on this film. Born Jewish, in what is now Romania, Bronston changed his name from Bronstein to Bronston when he first came to Hollywood as a producer. During the 1950s, after he left Hollywood, he made many overtures and inroads to the Vatican. Bronston told the story, probably embellished, that he met the Pope one day walking down the street in Rome and struck up a friendship. At any rate, he became the Vatican Photographer, and combined his skills in photography to not only catalog the Church's art treasures but to make a documentary film about them.

Before production on *King of Kings* began, Bronston had an audience with Pope John XXIII and received some form of script approval. It would be a different re-telling of the story of Christ. Since the DeMille silent film, no motion picture had actually shown Christ's face, a show of reverence and a desire to not have an actor perceived in such a holy role. The Messiah was typically shown from the back, or as a shadow, or in a very long shot. Bronston determined that the film should document Christ's life, as well as the turbulent times he lived in. To do so meant that we had to see and hear the actor playing the role.

Originally, the director was to be John Farrow, who had worked on Bronston's previous *John Paul Jones*, but finally the job went to Nicholas Ray, a fiercely independent director of such films as *Rebel Without a Cause*, *Johnny Guitar*, and *The True Story of Jesse James*, which had Jeffrey Hunter in the cast.

The Story

Basically, the script follows a pastiche of well-known Bible stories, but adds on a layer that illuminates the times Jesus lived in. Much time is spent on the oppression by the Romans, and the Jews who wanted freedom and revolution.

The story opens with Orson Welles' narration, beautifully written by an uncredited Ray Bradbury.

It moves to Roman General Pompey (Conrado San Martin)

defiling the great Jewish Temple at Jerusalem, and then establishes the Romans as cruel and slothful.

The story changes focus to the Nativity, and pauses briefly on the early years of Jesus. It shows his temptation in the wilderness, then subsequently he gathers his disciples, as a subplot (not contained in the Bible) involves Barabbas (Harry Guardino) and Jesus' disciple Judas (Rip Torn) plotting to overthrow the Roman rule of Judea.

The miracles Jesus performed are hinted at rather than overtly shown.

Jesus delivers the Sermon on the Mount to thousands of people, in a question and answer form, the camera following him as he moves answering questions.

After the Last Supper, Jesus is arrested, and, again, at variance from the standard Bible stories, is put on trial before Pilate (Hurd Hatfield) with counsel from a Roman centurion (Ron Randall).

Pilate convicts Jesus, and frees Barabbas. Jesus is crucified, with director Ray's camera riding upward with Jesus as the cross is raised.

After the crucifixion, the disciples are collecting their fishing nets at the Sea of Galilee and see the resurrected Christ only as a shadow.

The Film

King of Kings was really Bronston's first mega-epic in his quartet of big films. It showcased a lot of location filming, large constructed sets, the proverbial cast of thousands, consisting of the Spanish Army and extras hired from villages that surrounded the shooting locations.

Cameras rolled on April 24, 1960, but pre-production work began almost two years before. Bronston rented two of Spain's largest studios for interiors, Sevilla and Chamartin in Madrid. George Wakhevitch was lured from Paris to do the costumes and the sets. Like Bronston, Wakhevitch was born in Russia. He had designed dozens of operas and many French films. This was his only film with the Bronston organization.

Studio publicity said Spain was chosen for the locations because it most resembled the holy land of 2,000 years ago. The reality was that Bronston was headquartered in Spain. He had the availability of cheap labor, and large casts. Spain had hosted and would host many epic films before and after *King of Kings*, because its geography, from plains to mountains to the Mediterranean, could look like any place. For the same reasons, Spain became the American West for almost two decades of Italian-produced Westerns.

The studio claimed 396 sets were built, overflowing the two main studios. There were also eight locations to deal with, including Chinchon near Madrid for the Sermon on the Mount, El Fresno for the Jordan River, Navacerrada was Golgotha, Lago Alberche became the Sea of Galilee and Manzanares was dressed as Nazareth. The Temple of Judea at the Sevilla studios was most impressive, with hundred-foot columns. Unfortunately, it blew down in a major windstorm. Months of work had been destroyed. Bronston surveyed the site, and ordered the set be rebuilt. It took three months, and added a good deal of cost to the film's budget.

Nicholas Ray was an interesting choice for the film. Starting in radio and then moving to film, he had an impressive string of *film noir* titles like *They Live by Night, In a Lonely Place* and *On Dangerous Ground*. Many of his films featured characters who were young outsiders, such as in *Rebel Without a Cause*, a theme repeated in *King of Kings*. He was also noted for his bold use of color, and his emphasis on architecture, perhaps growing out of his youthful studies working under Frank Lloyd Wright. Both of those traits are very clear in *King of Kings*. His use of bright costumes (even putting Jesus in a red cloak) and his creative use of space and the wide-screen Technirama frame are notable.

The film was originally titled *Son of Man* and was a loose-knit series of tableaux from the Bible. Screenwriter Philip Yordan and Ray crafted the story as far more political, with the plotting by the Judeans against Rome carrying almost as much story weight as the story of Jesus. They were assisted by a Catholic Priest, Rev. George Kilpatrick, who was present during much of the production.

The production, like many of the Bronston films, was chaotic. It was near the beginning of the soon to be ugly relationship with Pierre DuPont, who was providing financial guarantees.

Alan Brown, one of the film's co-producers, said Bronston, as always, was living day by day. "Sam was a real genius. He was a salesman, including using tears. Say he had $500,000. He'd have the contract of [Sophia] Loren, the promise of Pierre DuPont, and he would build a magnificent set, which he would bring the distributors to see. He'd have no script. Sam took them in legitimately, those people who think they're geniuses. But the financing was always the worst, tense time for Sam. He would have just enough money to get through till Tuesday, and it was already Wednesday. I used to keep money on *King of Kings* in a Kleenex box - pesetas with a Kleenex on top; hidden for emergency because Sam was in London or Zurich." [Quoted in *Nicholas Ray* by Bernard Eisenschitz]

To add to the confusion, MGM was interested in investing, largely because they saw the film as a possible threat to *Ben-Hur*, which was still in theaters. With MGM money, of course, came the confusion of who was really in charge of the picture. MGM inserted its head of production, Sol Siegel, into the mix. Siegel had joined MGM after years with Republic, Paramount and 20th Century-Fox. He joined MGM in 1956 and became vice president in charge of production in 1958. Clearly, Siegel had his own ideas about how *King of Kings* should unfold. He felt the film was too long, needed more action, and had a weak ending. (Given that the film ends with the resurrection, one wonders what Siegel would have preferred as an ending.)

With MGM in the mix, Ray began to lose control of the film, and the production environment became chaotic. MGM wanted a new character in the film, played by British actor Richard Johnson (*Khartoum, Zulu*). Johnson's role as "David" was to function as a bridge between major plot threads. He was a Jewish Zealot torn between the teachings of Jesus, Roman law, and the violent resistance of Barabbas. Despite his being in many scenes, they were later removed during the extended editing process and only a glimpse of Johnson remains in the Good Friday scenes as Jesus enters the Holy Temple.

A side note: Bronston always invited throngs of people to see his sets and watch the movie in production. Hoping for publicity, Bronston invited TV talk show host Jack Paar and his family to visit the set. Paar's daughter Randy was instantly given a part as an extra in the film, and her out-of-place blonde hair can be seen fleetingly during the Palm Sunday scenes. Paar, of course, showed his home movies of the production on his late night TV show, giving Bronston some free publicity.

Following the pattern of many Bronston films, the actual production was rife with intrigue. Unfortunately, Ray's creativity was often compromised by behind-the-scenes power struggles. According to Gavin Lambert, a Ray associate, in Eisenschitz's biography of Ray, "The atmosphere was really evil: it was like two courts . . . Nick and Phil Yordan, who had been old friends, were not speaking. Yordan was executively above Nick, so he was there not only as a writer, but to see that Nick shot his script. And it was like an arena, these battlements, this enormous open air set. There was the court of Nick at one end, and the court of Yordan way over at the other, and they communicated only by walkie-talkie radio, they never spoke a word directly. 'I wonder what they're up to down there,' Nick would say, 'I wonder what they're plotting . . . but I'm going to sneak in a few things . . . '"

With so many scenes removed, it was felt that narration was needed to tie the disparate elements of the film together, so Ray visited Ray Bradbury in Los Angeles and asked for help. Bradbury was well liked and well known in Hollywood, and had done an acclaimed screenplay for John Huston's 1956 film *Moby Dick*.

Bradbury told me they needed compelling narration for the film, and what Bradbury delivered was moving and memorable. Bradbury's narration, spoken by Orson Welles, gives the first scenes in the film gravity and poetry: "Thus, for more than fifty years after Pompey's invasion, the history of Judea could be read by the light of burning towns. If gold was not the harvest, there was a richness of people to be gathered. The battalions of Caesar Augustus brought in the crop. Like sheep from their own green fields, the Jews went to the slaughter. They went from the stone quarries to build Rome's triumphal arches. But Caesar could find no Jew to press Rome's laws on this fallen land, so Caesar named one, Herod the Great, an Arab of the Bedouin tribe, as the new, false, and maleficent King of the Jews. But from the dust at Herod's feet, rebellions of Jews rose up, and Herod in reply planted evil seeds from which forests of Roman crosses grew high of Jerusalem's Hills. And Herod the great, passing pleased, bade the forest multiply."

According to Bradbury, "Yordan did not want myself or Orson credited." Memos from the time of the production claim Orson wanted equal billing to star Jeffrey Hunter, or no credit at all. Welles got the latter. The issue of their credits must have been decided late in production, because Bradbury told me he retains a few frames of filmstrip with his name on it.

Bradbury was also asked to help fix the end of the film, probably due to the complaining of Sol Siegel. Bradbury suggested to Ray that if he was stuck for an ending to try reading the Bible. Ray and the others pressed Bradbury for something more, something unique. Bradbury told me, "I conceived an ending where the ghost of Jesus became visible to the disciples who were gathering their nets on the shore of a lake. Jesus tells them to go into the world and preach the Gospel, then as Jesus walks toward the horizon he appears to be elevated from the ground as in a mirage similar to what you see when it appears water is on a road on a hot day. As he continues to walk, only his footprints are visible, and then they are covered with blowing dust. Then the scene cuts to the disciples' footprints, which are also covered in blowing dust and the film closes." After all the effort, Nicholas Ray told Bradbury such a scene would be too expensive to film, and they wound up with a simplified version of it that did not require complicated optical effects.

Bradbury's scripting of the narration led to an offer to do *The Greatest Story Ever Told* for George Stevens. Instead, Bradbury told me he suggested Carl Sandburg, who did wind up contributing to the script. Bradbury told me he thought *The Greatest Story Ever Told* is the better film, largely because Stevens directed it and that it was visually stunning.

Still, in all, Bradbury is proud of his work on *King of Kings*. He was in Hollywood for some of the post--production dubbing, and met many members of the cast. He thinks to this day it was a good film about a difficult subject.

The History
Since there is and always will be debate over the origins and history of the time as told by the Bible, this is something that can't be settled easily here. Suffice to say that *King of Kings* is not a literal retelling of any of the four books of the New Testament, but rather a story that blends aspects of each into a new story. It layers on top of that a political tale turning Barabbas into a Judean revolutionary firebrand instead of a simple thief as described in the Bible stories. It begins, not at the Nativity, where most Christian stories start, but rather in a summary of the politics of the time.

In retrospect, *King of Kings* is about the least "religious" of all of the movies about Christ. Miracles are hinted at or talked about by characters in reports to Herod and Pilate, and even the resurrected Christ is just a shadow on a beach. This may have been an attempt to please everyone across all religious faiths, even skeptics. It may have been Yordan, and to some extent Ray, but whatever the reason, the story does not have a deep well of religious feeling as much as it plays out the story of a lonely man against a corrupt society, a common theme in Ray's work.

Interestingly, Bronston's son Bill believes the film was squarely aimed at Catholics. "They labored in order to nail that one down because they had a real problem in getting papal signoff, and they needed to have that Christian market, that Catholic market guaranteed at the front end. It was very important for them to cut those deals, to create all that promotional material that would be part of the merchandising connected to the movie. Now, compared to today, it was nothing but in those days it was very creative. They knew that they were going to really market *King of Kings*. This movie was made for a Catholic audience. A locked Catholic audience."

Even so, Bill Bronston knew that his dad had to make a movie that appealed to a wider slice of the film-going public. "I think it was in part because of my dad, who had a real, real deep, abiding commercial sense of ecumenism. But I think this had to do with my dad's sense of general audience. He had a very, very concrete sense of his being an instrument for, and a beneficiary of, a general family audience. And he knew that this movie had to be ecumenical.

"That may have been why the Pope signed off on it because it's always very controversial as how you walk that line to tell that story, giving all the fanaticism and the craziness and the vested interest in the story. That was a very interesting struggle to get it right, to get that script right, to get the story right, to get the signoffs from the Pope, because they had to have papal imprimatur to go with it. I assure you that all of the investments that were made during the time when he shot the Vatican in those old days were dealt up and used in terms of his familiarity with the Vatican, the fact that he had done this major work for them before, when he was coming out of Catholic Spain he really worked to try and create something."

The film has some major set pieces, the most impressive perhaps being the Sermon on the Mount, which was, in fact, the Sermon on the Mountain. After searching the Spanish countryside, Ray selected a spot in an olive grove in the rolling hills of Venta de Frascuela, about 30 miles southeast of Madrid.

Ray believed that Christ would have had to move among the crowd at the historic sermon, or no one would have been able to hear him. He conceived of a scene where Jesus would move among the crowd answering questions as was done in the traditional rabbinical style.

Of course, moving on a mountainside, while a camera weighting hundreds of pounds follows, is a difficult assignment. Even today, with lighter, more mobile equipment, this scene would be a difficult one. The production team came up with the idea of putting the heavy camera on tracks, but moving the camera would have been difficult, so a complicated counterweight system was designed and more tracks were laid on the other side of the mountain. Then the camera, in rough balance, could be easily moved along those tracks to follow the action as Jeffrey Hunter moved among the crowds.

To make the scene work, 160 feet of camera tracks were placed on one side of the mountain, and another 160 feet were placed on the side away from where the action would be. The incline of the mountain was roughly 58 degrees, so the shots gave the scene a compelling ambiance, with the camera seeming to effortlessly go up and down the mountainside following Jeffrey Hunter as he walked among the crowd. Seven thousand villagers participated in the scene, and Ray was impressed with the reverence shown by these amateur actors.

The Cast

The role of Christ is an impossible one. Many people were considered, among them Max Von Sydow (who wound up playing Christ in *The Greatest Story Ever Told* in 1965), Christopher Plummer (*The Fall of the Roman Empire*), Peter Cushing and Tom Fleming. The idea to hire Jeffrey Hunter apparently came from John Ford, who suggested him to Ray based on his performance in *The Searchers*. Ray knew Hunter, as he had directed him in *The True Story of Jesse James*. Bronston eagerly agreed to the casting choice. "I really chose him for his eyes," Bronston said. "It was important that the man playing Christ have memorable eyes. The film was a great responsibility. We did not permit Hunter to be interviewed or photographed because the part had to be portrayed in a reverent manner."

It was important for Bronston and his team to keep the ages of Christ and other players close to their stated biblical ages. Hunter was 34 when filming began. Brigid Bazlen, who played Salome, was an appropriate 16. Rip Torn, who played Judas, was 30.

Hunter took the role very seriously, but said during production that he was not fully aware of the impact of the role until the filming of the Sermon on the Mount sequence. "There were some seven thousand extras gathered from surrounding villages - simple devout country folk. When I appeared in my robes, I saw to my astonishment that many dropped to their knees and made the sign of the cross as I passed by.

"They knew perfectly well, of course, that I was merely an actor playing a part. Still, I was a living representation of a figure they had regarded from childhood with most sacred awe. It was then that I realized what I had undertaken. I felt it even more deeply as the film went along and do so even more now, long after I have shed His robes."

As production continued, Hunter noticed a similar effect spreading to the cast and crew. "At first there seemed to be timidity, and then complete withdrawal of the usual banter and fun making on the set. Seldom did anyone engage me in personal conversations. Eventually, I simply went in my dressing room between scenes, resting and studying my lines until the cameras were ready."

In an interview after production completed, Hunter reflected on the role. "I was warned not to do it, actors who play Jesus are supposed to have a hard time getting other roles to follow, but I felt it was a myth. After all, how can you be typecast as Christ? There just aren't that many Jesus roles around. If it affected my career at all, I think it helped it."

He was also asked if, as reported, he stopped drinking and smoking during production. He answered, "To a certain degree I did. You try to get the feel of any role, but it's more difficult in the case of Jesus Christ because everyone has their own personal image of Him. It's a role you take on, knowing that no matter how you play it; you are going to disappoint many."

Hunter's career was a short one, and being in *King of Kings* did not seem to enhance it. After appearing in many TV series and in a few movies including *A Guide for the Married Man* and *Custer of the West* (produced by Philip Yordan) Hunter was filming *Viva America!* in Spain when an explosion on the set came too close to the actor. Almost immediately he began complaining of dizziness and headaches. On May 27, 1969, Hunter had a cerebral hemorrhage and fell down the steps in his home. He died shortly after emergency surgery at age 42.

Originally, many big name actors were pursued for parts, including Richard Burton, John Gielgud and James Mason (who later worked for Bronston on *The Fall of the Roman Empire*), but one by one they dropped out, citing either other commitments or lack of interest in the script. These remaining roles were filled in with solid actors.

Robert Ryan, an old friend of Ray's, played John the Baptist, giving the role some power and freshness. Ryan had worked in other MGM films, including *Bad Day at Black Rock*, and had worked with Ray in the classic *On Dangerous Ground* (1952), where he played a bitter and violent policeman. Other notable roles included *The Naked Spur, Billy Budd, The Professionals, The Longest Day, Battle of the Bulge* and *The Wild Bunch*. He died of lung cancer in 1973.

Siobhan McKenna played the part of the Virgin Mary. A distinguished Irish actress, she was a member of Dublin's famed Abbey Players. In her career, she was nominated twice for Tony Awards for best actress, and worked in the legitimate theater as well as in film. Notable film appearances included *Playboy of the Western World, Of Human Bondage*, and *Doctor Zhivago*. She died in 1986 of lung cancer.

Hurd Hatfield took on the role of Pontius Pilate. A New York actor, he appeared on stage, movies and TV. He has well known for playing the title role in the Oscar-winning *The Picture of Dorian Gray* in 1945. After *King of Kings*, he was cast by Bronston in *El Cid*. Notable screen appearances included *Harlow* and *Mickey One*. He was frequently cast in television series, including *Voyage to the Bottom of the Sea, Kojak, Knight Rider*, and *Murder, She Wrote*. Hatfield died in 1998 of a heart attack.

Lucius the Centurion was played by Ron Randall, an Australian actor. Other film roles included a lead in *The Most Dangerous Man Alive, The World of Suzie Wong*, along with TV appearances in *Mission: Impossible, The Farmer's Daughter* and *Bewitched*. In 1966 Randall appeared with Robert Taylor in *Savage Pampas*, a Western-style adventure filmed in Argentina. It was produced by Bronston associate Jamie Prades, and, although not credited, Bronston himself was involved as a producer as well. Randall died in 2005 from complications following a stroke.

Harry Guardino played Barabbas. Considered a powerful actor at the time, he was noticed by the Bronston organization after his performance in *5 Branded Women* (1960). Guardino was good at playing tough cops as well as crooks. He appeared on many television shows, including *Dr. Kildare, Hawaii Five-0, Checkmate, Route 66, Naked City, Police Story* and *Murder, She Wrote*. He died of lung cancer in 1995.

Herod Antipas was played by veteran Australian character actor Frank Thring. He had played Pontius Pilate in *Ben-Hur*. He had also appeared in *The Vikings* with Kirk Douglas and Tony Curtis. He worked for Bronston again playing a Moor in *El Cid*, and did much television work both in the U.S. and Australia. Thring died of cancer in 1994.

Rip Torn played Judas. He had appeared on Broadway in Tennessee Williams' *Sweet Bird of Youth*. Film roles included *Baby Doll, A Face in the Crowd* and *Pork Chop Hill*. Still actively acting today, Torn has recently appeared in *Defending Your Life, Canadian Bacon, Men in Black*, and many television appearances over the years, including *Naked City, Columbo, Kojak, The Larry Sanders Show* and *Will and Grace*.

Brigid Bazlen took the role of Salome. Born in Wisconsin, she was 16 when she made *King of Kings*. She had been cast as the Blue Fairy on a Chicago TV station when she was 14. Bazlen made *The Honeymoon Machine* in 1961 just after her role in the Bronston film, and followed it with a small role in *How the West Was Won*. That ended her acting career except for a stint on the television soap opera *Days of Our Lives*. She died in Seattle in 1989 of cancer.

The Music

The score for the film was done by the great composer Miklos Rozsa. A three-time Oscar winner, Rozsa almost single-handedly "invented" the sound of Roman music for the 1951 film *Quo Vadis?* Combining Hebrew themes with surviving Greek music, which Rozsa felt were the largest influences on the Romans, he gave the Roman Empire a "sound" that he was able to use again in *Ben-Hur* and again in *King of Kings*.

He was not excited to do another Roman film just after *Ben-Hur*, especially one that dealt with many of the same characters in the same time frame. His daughter, Juliet Rozsa-Brown, explained the issue in a recent BBC interview. "*King of Kings* was not his favorite film. He found that doing the film right after doing *Ben-Hur* that this was one of the toughest assignments he had. In his book, *A Double Life*, he says, 'Just before I left for my summer holiday in 1959, the studio – meaning MGM – asked me to go to Madrid. It seemed that an independent producer, Samuel Bronston, was producing a picture there and MGM thought I should do the music. Having just done a picture in which Jesus played a supporting role I was dumbfounded to learn that the new film was *King of Kings* in which he was the star. But at that time I had apparently become the musical expounder of the ancient world par excellence, and I agreed.'

"The main problem was to write new music to exactly the same themes and scenes as those in *Ben-Hur* – 'The Nativity,' 'The Way of the Cross,' 'Golgotha,' 'the Resurrection.' It was a tough job."

In a BBC interview after the *King of Kings* release, Rozsa had more to say. "There were all the great scenes which I had to do again and, obviously, differently. I have no intention to compare myself with Michelangelo but imagine that after Michelangelo has worked years and years on the Last Judgment in the Sistine Chapel, the Pope would have asked him to decorate another chapel, also with a same theme but entirely different."

Rozsa knew the music would be extremely important to the film. Jesse Kaye, a producer at MGM Records, had unwanted advice to the composer, as Rozsa told the story in a BBC interview: "Music is a very important and integral element of the whole thing. There are films where so-called commercial tunes would do very well. As a matter of fact, I had a meeting with a gentleman from MGM Records and he said, 'I'll tell you what's the trouble with you.' I said, 'Well do, because I'd like to know.' And he said, 'You write too many themes.' I said, 'Do I really?' He said, 'Yes, I have counted *King of Kings*, you had twelve themes in it.' I said, 'Did I really? I'm glad to hear that.' He said, 'No, no. I don't mean it that way. You should have one theme. And today we need just one melody and plug it from the beginning to the end.' I said, 'Look, this is very good for the record business but I am not in the record business. I am a part of the picture business. My duty is to make this picture better, not to sell songs, not to sell records. That's your business.'

He said, 'Yes, but we had a picture that had one tune and it sold much more than your *Ben-Hur* records.' I said, 'In that case I am in the wrong business and you are in the right one.'"

The picture was immensely improved by Rozsa's music. Early in the production process Rozsa was troubled by what he considered the film's "nonsensical biblical goulash" [Rozsa in his autobiography, *A Double Life*]

More troubling was doing Salome's famous dance for Herod. "The studio had told me not to try to discuss the dance with Bronston. When we got to Madrid, I tried the writer but he was very evasive and quickly left town. The director was even more vague. When pressed he told me that the choreographer was his wife. She had once been a dancer with Hermes Pan who had staged many musicals and though she'd never done any choreography before she felt she could do this. Bronston had found his Salome in Chicago. She was a schoolgirl of about 16, a bit plump, who somewhat surprisingly had never acted or danced before. I was almost in tears. Here was a choreographer who had never choreographed and a dancer who had never danced. I finished my piece, about six or seven minutes long, and was practicing it on a piano in the basement of the Hilton where we were staying, so as to be able to play it for the lady choreographer. When I finished there was a huge burst of applause. The kitchen staff had all come to listen. This was to be my only popular success in Madrid." [From *A Double Life*]

As the film was edited, the sequence was shortened so that Salome (played by Bridgid Bazlen) did not have to dance at all, and only ran between temple pillars on the set.

The music, despite Rozsa's fears, was excellent and was nominated for a Golden Globe. The music and narration bridges written by Ray Bradbury go a long way to tie the film's sequences together.

More important, to Rozsa certainly, was that the score did not seem to be a rehash of *Ben-Hur* but went off into some fresh musical directions that have made the score popular to this day. The expanded CD version is still in the catalog from Rhino Records. It includes all 140 minutes of the music Rozsa wrote for the film. In addition, choral groups around the world continue to perform music from the film in churches and concerts.

Reviews and Box Office

There was a great deal of controversy about the film, in particular the decision to show the face of Christ, which had generally been avoided in biblical films. (In *Ben-Hur*, the face of Christ is never clearly seen; even in the more recent *Barabbas* a bright sun obscures Christ's features.) In *The Greatest Story Ever Told*, which followed *King of Kings*, George Stevens showcased actor Max von Sydow, who, as I have mentioned, had also been considered to play Jesus by Bronston and Ray.

Bronston also fought off criticism, particularly rabid in England, as to why a Jew should be making a movie about Christ.

The film opened to very good box office, and *Variety* and the European trade press were reporting that advance bookings were exceeding those for *Ben-Hur*. The film eventually grossed 25 million dollars worldwide.

The *New York Times* admired the restraint in the film, but found much to dislike as well, and reviewer Bosley Crowther noticed how much of the religiosity of the story had been stripped out. "Mr. Yordan and/or Mr. Ray have missed or disguised certain happenings that were dramatic and important in Jesus' life. They have obfuscated the healings, avoided the miracles and skipped altogether the judgment of Jesus as a blasphemer and seditionist by the Jews. They have passed Him along directly from Judas' kiss to

Pontius Pilate's court and have there made His trial a tedious colloquy between Pilate and a Roman centurion.

"In short, the essential drama of the messianic issue has been missed and the central character has been left to perform quietly in a series of collateral tableaux.

"Mr. Hunter wears his makeup nobly and performs with simplicity and taste, which is more than can be said for some others. Hurd Hatfield plays Pilate haughtily, Robert Ryan makes a shaggy John the Baptist and Ron Randell is a curt centurion.

"Harry Guardino's Barabbas is a howling barbarian and Frank Thring as Herod Antipas is a grimacing and gaudy grotesque. Rip Torn as Judas Iscariot, Brigid Bazlen as Salome and Siobhan McKenna as Mary shine variously in a large cast.

"Of it all, let us say the spirit is hinted but the projection of it is weak. The 'greatest story' has not yet been captured for its full dramatic impact on the screen."

Other reviews praised the sets, which always happen to a Bronston film, and either praised Hunter's restrained performance or complained about his strangely hairless body and out of place blue eyes. Of course, it was Bronston's casting decision that chose Hunter because of his eyes.

Variety liked *King of Kings*, finding it tasteful and artistic: "*King of Kings* wisely substitutes characterizations for orgies. Director Nicholas Ray has brooded long and wisely upon the meaning of his meanings, has planted plenty of symbols along the path, yet avoided the banalities of religious calendar art.

"The sweep of the story presents a panorama of the conquest of Judea and its persistent rebelliousness, against which the implication of Christ's preachments assume, to pagan Roman overlords, the reek of sedition. All of this is rich in melodrama, action, battle and clash. But author Philip Yordan astutely uses the bloodthirsty Jewish patriots, unable to think except in terms of violence, as telling counterpoint to the Messiah's love-one-another creed.

"Jeffrey Hunter's blue orbs and auburn bob (wig, of course) are strikingly pictorial. The handling of the Sermon on the Mount which dominates the climax of the first part before intermission is wonderfully skillful in working masses of people into an alternation of faith and skepticism while cross-cutting personal movement among them of the Saviour and his disciples."

Final Thoughts

King of Kings made good money, looked stunning on screen, and has Ray's trademark conflicts and splashes of color used to further story points. It is interesting that MGM had no further interest in Bronston after the film premiered, and Allied Artists distributed his next film, *El Cid*.

King of Kings is a worthy entertainment, but was not the deeply religious experience some theatergoers craved. It was an amalgam of Nicholas Ray's trying to tell an old story in a new pictorial way, and Bronston's desire to mount an epic for audiences that seemed to be craving them. The script is strangely devoid of heavy religious mythology. Almost all of the miracles are unseen; they are dealt with in a report delivered by Lucius to Pilate. This was in keeping with what Yordan and Ray were trying to accomplish, but left the more devout a bit chilly. What the filmmakers were trying to do was create a film that worked for the devout, but could also work for a more skeptical, modern audience. It could be said that *King of Kings* missed the mark at both ends, but many critics found the film properly restrained and still moving.

Standout scenes are the entrance of Pompey into the Temple; the slaughter of the Jews; the Sermon on the Mount, with the previously mentioned camera movements up and down the mountain; the Last Supper, staged in a fresh way that avoided the usual clichés; and the crucifixion, with a camera mounted on the top of the cross looking down at Jeffrey Hunter as the cross is raised into position. Also notable is Jesus' trial, as he stands silently while Pilate and his appointed counsel Lucius debate the charges. It does not follow the biblical form of the story, but was dramatically powerful nevertheless.

While only partially successful as art, it made money and pushed Bronston ahead toward *El Cid* and his other epic stories.

Like many of the Bronston films that were to come, there are transcendent themes: a man alone against great odds, an attempt by the main character to communicate a worthy message to a power structure that turned a deaf ear.

As in his later films, Bronston was part of the process, deciding to a degree what stayed in the film and what came out. *King of Kings* was hurt because of MGM's constant fiddling with the script. They insisted on added plot threads that they later took out, and there is a jumpy quality to the parts of the film that can be attributed to that interference.

Looking back on *King of Kings*, the picture holds up very well. There is a lot of Nicholas Ray in the picture, from the aforementioned striking use of colors to his artistic use of the wide, Super Technirama frame. There are inspiring moments. It may have lacked the visual impact of later films like George Stevens' *The Greatest Story Ever Told*, but it also avoided much of the corn and severe miscasting that Stevens' film suffered from.

Its sense of political reality and conflict of the time is palpable. *King of Kings* was a film about great ideas taking root in a hostile land. It previewed the themes that would be explored in *El Cid, 55 Days at Peking* and *The Fall of the Roman Empire*. More than 45 years later it is still shown on TV and unlike many of the Bronston films that are out of circulation, *King of Kings* is able to constantly renew and re-engage a fresh audience from year to year. It is the only Bronston film available to film buffs at this writing, but that will change with the release of the the rest of the Bronston epics by Weinstein likely in 2008. *King of Kings* is a beautifully mastered DVD that preserves Rosza's stirring score as well as the striking cinema-tography that were trademarks of all the Bronston productions.

El Cid

"As Big as Ben-Hur *if not Bigger."* —
promotional tag line

Released in 1961;   **Director**: Anthony Mann; **Producer**: Samuel Bronston; **Screenplay**: Frederic M. Frank, Philip Yordan and Ben Barzman (originally uncredited); **Cinematography**: Robert Krasker; **Music**: Miklos Rozsa; **Cast**: Charlton Heston, Sophia Loren, John Fraser, Raf Vallone, Genevieve Page, Herbert Lom; Running time: **Released**: Allied Artists; **Running time**: 3:04; Theatrical Aspect Ratio: 2.35:1

El Cid is one of the greatest epic films ever produced. It's also generally regarded as the best film the Bronston organization ever made, and it remains in many people's memories as an all time favorite movie. If Bronston had made no other movie in his career, it would have been enough to guarantee him lasting fame. It has heroism, romance, epic battles, and art direction that put the film in very rare company. Its decade's long absence from the home video scene in North America has made it even more desirable and cherished. In short, *El Cid* is unforgettable, and it was the financial engine that allowed the empire Samuel Bronston created to produce more historical epics.

It is unlikely such a film mounted this way could ever be made again. The cost of cast, sets and costumes would simply be too prohibitive. The recent film *Kingdom of Heaven,* directed by Ridley Scott, takes place in a similar period of history, but as epic as the film is, most of the armies are digital creations and the sets are mostly done with computer graphics. It also doesn't have the emotional core that *El Cid* has.

Samuel Bronston dreamed of making this kind of film for many years. For Bronston, it was a way to be free of Hollywood and studio politics. For this man, who as a youngster had only the loose change in his pockets, *El Cid* was the dream come alive. More than 45 years after its production, it is still breathtaking.

El Cid tells the story of the national hero of Spain, loved and despised by his wife-to-be, honored, exiled and reunited with his king. It is a story of overcoming great odds while keeping one's integrity. It is a story a thousand years old, and yet, like most timeless classics, a story for today.

The Story

Rodrigo de Bivar (Heston) is on his way to his wedding, and releases some Islamic Moors he and his men have captured after the Moors burned a Christian village. Their release is contingent upon pledging loyalty to King Ferdinand, which they do. The Moors, finding him courageous and lenient, name him "El Cid," or "lord."

An immediate controversy erupts, as a representative of the King wants the Moors hanged, not released, and charges Rodrigo with treason. The issue is brought before the King, and Rodrigo is accused of treason by his soon-to-be father-in-law, Count Gormaz (Andrew Cruickshank), who is also the King's Champion. Rodrigo's father argues this charge, and is insulted and slapped by the Count. Rodrigo avenges this insult by asking Gormaz to forgive his father and retract the charge, saying, "What man can live without honor?" When Gormaz rebuffs him, Rodrigo unsheathes his sword, the result of which is a dramatic fight, and the death of Count Gormaz. Chimene (Sophia Loren), Rodrigo's bride-in-waiting, has promised her dying father to avenge his murder.

At this moment, enemies of the King want to take advantage of the fallen Gormaz and fight for the city of Calahorra. King Ferdinand (Ralph Truman) protests that he has no champion, and Rodrigo offers to take up the gauntlet, saying that God can judge his guilt or innocence by the outcome of a joust that will determine who will rule the city.

On the field of Calahorra, Rodrigo triumphs over Don Martin (Christopher Rhodes) and then, after having become a hero for the King and his court, tries to repair the damage with Chimene, but her hatred won't let her forgive.

King Ferdinand dies, and his sons are warring for land and influence. The Cid wants no part of the battle between Sancho (Gary Raymond) and Alfonso (John Fraser), but Sancho is killed by a dagger in the back.

Returning to Castile, Rodrigo is asked for help by Alfonso, but humiliating him before his court, forces the King to swear he had no hand in Sancho's death. Alfonso takes the oath, but filled with humiliation and hatred, banishes Rodrigo and ceases his land and property, then arrests Chimene and the children and places them in a dungeon.

El Cid takes the city of Valencia, and refuses the crown, selflessly taking the city for Alfonso, despite their differences.

The Cid, now controlling Valencia awaits a large attack by Almorovid Moors from North Africa led by Ben Yussef (Herbert Lom). In the first wave, the Cid is hit with an arrow in his upper chest, and breaks the arrow off at the shank. He tells Chimene, who has escaped with the help of Count Ordonez (Raf Vallone) and his closest aides, that he must lead the next morning's charge against the Moors "alive or dead."

Meanwhile, Alfonso appears and makes peace with Rodrigo, but, ever loyal, Rodrigo will not let the king bow down to him.

As the battle begins the next day, the Cid has died, and he is lashed to his horse in his armor. He rides out in a burst of organ music to meet the shocked invaders who thought the Cid was dead. The Cid's horse rides through Ben Yussef's defenses and into history. The Cid has created the beginnings of the united country of Spain out of warring Kings and centuries of internal and external strife.

The Film

Released in 1961 at a cost of 6.25 million dollars, El Cid looked even more expensive on screen. Director Anthony Mann said at the time he thought it would have cost 20 million dollars to shoot the movie in the United States.

Martin Scorsese, who restored the film for a limited 1993 re-release through Miramax, said, "El Cid is one of the greatest epic films ever made. Anthony Mann's sense of composition, his use of space, and his graceful camera movements bring to life an ancient tapestry where the transformation of an ordinary man into a legend become almost a mystical experience."

To many, including this writer, the film has a passion and pageantry unmatched by films of the period or since. Cinematography by Australian Robert Krasker (Henry V, The Third Man, Billy Budd, Alexander the Great, The Collector), a stirring score by Miklos Rozsa (Spellbound, Ben-Hur, The Lost Weekend, Quo Vadis?), and castles, sweeping landscapes filled with armies on horseback, and intricate and accurate set designs combine for an experience that can truly be described as magical.

To add to the epic feel, the film was shot in Super Technirama 70, a format which ran 35mm film through the camera horizontally. It created a very large negative eight perforations wide and also incorporated 150% anamorphic compression. Bronston's *King of Kings* and *Circus World* were also shot in the process.

There really *is* a magic in *El Cid*. It starts, perhaps, with the symmetry of its opening and closing scenes. Rodrigo breaks arrows off a statue of Christ, arrows that belonged to the Moors as they destroyed a church. It's echoed near the finale, when the Cid breaks off the arrow he has been shot with, so he will have the strength to ride with his men during the defense of Valencia. It's a touch that may be missed by many, but it indicates the care of scripting and overall conception of this epic among epics. I asked Norma Barzman, wife of the late screenplay writer Ben Barzman, how conscious Ben was of these subtleties, and she said they were never accidental and were frequent in his best work.

When it was released, *El Cid* did excellent box office business, bringing in 26½ million dollars in the U.S. alone and more millions overseas. It was one of the top box office draws in 1961.

The film represented the Bronston organization at the top of its game, when director, actors, writers and craftsmen and women were able to execute a motion picture that inspired and thrilled and is remembered fondly more than four decades after its release.

El Cid weathered many challenges from the earliest days of pre-production. Orson Welles was cast in a supporting role, and then dropped in favor of Herbert Lom. Sophia Loren was cast as the female lead, then dropped, then she was back in again after scheduling problems were surmounted by her being on set for only 10 weeks. Scriptwriters were hired, including Frederick M. Frank, who had worked on *The Ten Commandments* for DeMille, and the final script was the result of then-uncredited writer Ben Barzman, who was living in Europe after being blacklisted in Hollywood.

The director chosen by the Bronston team was Anthony Mann, a well-respected director who had come to prominence with violent stylistic films like *T-Men* and a series of Westerns with Jimmy Stewart, including *Winchester '73*, *The Man from Laramie*, and *Man of the West* with Gary Cooper.

Mann was excited to do the project. "The reason I wanted to make *El Cid* was the theme 'a man road out to victory dead on his horse.' I loved the concept of that ending. Everybody would love to do this in life." (From *Films and Filming* - 1964)

Historical Background

So how much of the film is history and how much is hokum? There was a real El Cid, but so much mythology grew up around him it is difficult to separate the legend from the scant history. Although the historical character of the Cid was well known in Spain as a national hero, he was almost completely unknown in North America, and Bronston's film put him into people's consciousness.

We know Rodgrigo de Bivar was born about 1044 and died in July of 1099 at Valencia in some histories, at home, near Burgos in others.

He was called El Cid Campeador. The "El Cid" title (Lord) came from the Moors whom he both battled and befriended as shown in the film. The "Campeador" title roughly means champion and it was granted by his Christian countrymen. Historical stories about Rodrigo de Bivar were scarce, yet he was the national hero of Spain, celebrated in countless poems and ballads.

The first known mention of Rodrigo was in "The Poem of El Cid," an epic ballad written in the 12th century, and the Latin *Historia Roderici*. There is also a detailed eyewitness account of the siege and battle at Valencia by an Arab historian, Ibn 'Alqamah. The screenwriters based some of their story on inspiration from a French play, *Le Cid* by Pierre Corneille (1606-84), written in 1636. It was considered Corneille's greatest work and was based on a 1621 play also called *Le Cid*. It adapted and extended incidents from the original poem. There is also an opera, *Le Cid*, based on the earlier plays by Jules Massenet, which premiered at the Paris Opera in 1885.

The Corneille play deals with the coming of age of Rodrigo. His father asks him to restore honor to the family by challenging El Cid's future father-in-law to a duel. This presents a challenge for the young man. If he fails to respond, his family faces humiliation. If he does, he puts his pending marriage at risk. The unfolding of this story and how it shapes his life made the play one of the most talked about and popular of its time.

Many threads from the 12th-century epic and the later dramatic works have made it into the film:

Rodrigo's father being a champion of King Ferdinand; an insult to Rodrigo's father that must be avenged in a duel with the father of his future bride; friction between Ferdinand's sons, Sancho and Alphonso, on how the kingdom would be divided; Rodrigo's banishment; Chimene being put in prison with her children; the Battle for Valencia with Rodrigo the victor; and The Cid's death and being placed on a horse to win a key battle by frightening the Moors to flee.

With a rich tapestry of fact and legend to work with, the screenwriters were able to embellish, re-order and give depth to the historical and mythological framework that already existed.

History was messier than fiction. The real Cid was a warrior for hire, and the Moors and Christians in what was to become Spain were not clearly delineated. At times, Christians and Moors fought together against other Christians and Moors. This blurring is somewhat visible in the film as Rodrigo frees some Moors, battles others, and then joins with Moors to free Valencia in the film's climatic battle.

The Cid himself, not surprisingly, was far more complicated than the character in the film. In Richard Fletcher's seminal book, *The Quest for El Cid,* it's clear that the Cid was not just a loyal Christian, but spent a good part of his adult life as a mercenary and fought side by side with Muslims.

From the earliest 12th-century works, here is a rough history of the Cid: Born in 1043 or 1044, the Cid's father Diego Lainez was a minor nobleman of Castile, but his mother was born of the aristocracy. The Cid was brought up during the rule of Ferdinand I, in the household of the oldest of the King's sons, Sancho. Upon his death, Ferdinand's other son, Alfonso, became King of Leon, while Sancho ruled Castile. The Cid was named Commander of the troops by Sancho in 1065, and together they defeated the moors at Zaragoza. The two Kings began to plot against one another during this period, and when Sancho died Alfonso became King of Castile as well as Leon. Continuing political difficulties with Alfonso led to the Cid being exiled in 1081. As a result, the Cid fought as a mercenary for both Moors and Christians. He seemed to repair some of his differences with Alfonso and was noted to be present at the King's court in 1087. From October 1092 to May 1094 he led the siege of Valencia. The resistance finally gave way and the Cid entered Valencia as its conqueror. The victory would be short lived. The Moors continued to press Valencia, and eventually King Alfonso found it too difficult to defend. He evacuated the city, and then ordered it to be burned. On May 5, 1102, the North African Moors took over the city again, occupying it until 1238. The Cid died on July 10, 1099. His body was taken to Castile and buried near Burgos, where a tomb cult arose.

Threads of this history are visible in the film, either simplified, or elaborated. But the true souls of the script were the romantic epics and legends that grew from these histories.

The Production

El Cid was the best film turned out by the Bronston organization. As filming commenced, on November 14, 1960, the money was there [see my chapter on Bronston and how his films were financed], along with the talent to pull off a film of this magnitude.

Director Anthony Mann had a successful track record, and excelled at films about heroes with troubled pasts. In the early stages of his career he had a series of *film noir* projects (*T-Men* in 1947 and *Border Incident* in 1949), followed by a long series of Westerns with deep psychological overtones, many with Jimmy Stewart. Mann was not a stranger to the epic, having directed the burning of Rome segments of *Quo Vadis?* (MGM, 1951) and started *Spartacus* (Universal, 1960), but left after only 17 days due to differences with star and producer Kirk Douglas.

Blacklisted writer Ben Barzman (1911-1989) had left America rather than identify and testify against fellow members of the Communist Party. He was drafted by Philip Yordan, who coordinated scripting in all the Bronston films, and had worked with Mann on two earlier films, *Reign of Terror* (1949) and *The Last Frontier* (1955). A scriptwriter himself, with an Oscar to his credit, Yordan recruited the writers and felt Barzman had the talent to turn out a literate and explosive story. On the credits, the writers listed are Frederick M. Frank and Yordan. Neither wrote a word for the finished film. It was not until 1999 that Barzman's name was properly put back in the credits by the Academy of Motion Pictures Arts and Sciences.

Barzman's wife, Norma, told me that Ben read the original

script from Frank and it was unusable. Sophia Loren rejected it as well. Norma said Ben was asked if he could just use parts of the script and he replied, "No, I couldn't. I would have to start from scratch and that's impossible now." Barzman then added, "This was Friday, you're going to start shooting Monday. I can't. I told Tony Mann, I read it on the plane. I told him that I can't fix it."

Barzman then got hold of the French play about the Cid by Cornielle, and quickly fashioned the scenes with Rodrigo and the conflict with Chimene's father, Court Gomaz.

Norma Barzman says the production was in such a hurry for script pages a young boy was posted outside the door waiting for Ben to provide the badly needed story. "And he sat in the hallway, there was a little hallway to Ben's … Ben had a suite, sort of a sitting room and a bedroom. And toward the door this little boy sat and he waited for pages. And as soon as Ben had about four pages he would take them, get on his motorcycle and zoom out to the studio. That's how it was done. He got the play from the French consul on Saturday, and he was reading Corneille and he was fiddling with it. Monday morning he had a few pages for the boy and I got in on about Wednesday. I saw the way things were going. Then I started reading the pages, but I generally didn't have time to read the pages. I'm serious. Because the boy, if I was too long, he said, 'We can't, we can't, there's a phone call and we've got to get there.' It was like that."

In addition to the influence of the Cornielle play, the film has a historic thread, largely through the efforts of Juan Menendez Pidal, considered the best expert on Spain in Medieval times and the most respected authority on the Cid. While all his views on the Cid are not 100% accepted by historians today, he was a commanding presence during production of *El Cid* and kept the film on a historical track, letting Barzman fill in the gaps - of which there were many.

Charlton Heston played the lead, and here he was no Ben-Hur-lite. Heston got deeply into the role, soaking up the history of this real, rather than fictional, character. It was the fact that the Cid actually existed that began to excite Heston about the role, and in future films he would many times play famous characters from history. He studied books on the Cid and 11th-century Spain. He met with the film's historical advisor, and when on location he soaked up the culture the Cid lived in. Although in his journals and later interviews, Heston thought the film would have been better if William Wyler (*Ben-Hur*) directed it, many consider El Cid to be Heston's finest and most powerful role.

Sophia Loren was cast as Chimene, the lover and later wife of the Cid. Very young and unsure of herself at the time, she and Heston did not get along during the filming. Love scenes were difficult for both Loren and Heston, and in truth there was little chemistry between them off camera.

Barzman's script, while crackling with heroism and emotion, did not contain powerful love scenes, so another blacklisted writer, Bernard Gordon, told me he was asked to pen those parts of the story. "And they were all ready to go and typically they sent the script to Loren who was in Rome. She read it and said she wasn't going to make the picture. They were ready to go, you know. This happened all the time with us. So she said that she didn't even have one love scene. What was there for her to do? So [Philip] Yordan yanked me from what I was doing in Paris and said, 'Write me three or four love scenes for Loren and Heston.' Well, what the hell - he was paying me $1500 a week, which was a lot more than I made any other way, and I just took orders and I sat down and I wrote four scenes, about three or four pages each. Whatever love scenes there are in the picture I wrote. And they sent them to Loren and she said, OK, she'll do the picture, so I was a little bit of a hero at that point."

Gordon, who had a long association with Philip Yordan, went on to write *55 Days at Peking* and *Circus World* for Bronston. Working with Yordan in 1965 he wrote *Battle of the Bulge, Custer of the West*, and working independently he wrote *Krakatoa, East of Java*.

During the filming of *El Cid*, Heston came to resent Loren having what Heston perceived as her own writer, which added further tension. Also, as the script spans several years, Heston ages on screen, but Loren refused make up that would make her look older.

Norma Barzman, who was present during production while her late husband toiled over the script, told me there were great worries about the scenes between the two leads, particularly about Heston, who was difficult throughout the shoot. "Well, he kvetched [complained]! He kvetched about when she arrived. He thought it wasn't fair that he should be there so long and she should get away. But he was in every shot and it was ridiculous. His kvetches were nonsensical. Yes, he kvetched, but he also kvetched at the camera, the way he was shot that she got all the good ... but he was more beautiful.

"Heston was always such a pain in the neck on this set. Every time I went, actually, well, he was cold to me but that's not why. I mean, I watched him. He was awful with everybody. He wasn't likeable, he wasn't anything, and he was so worried about how he was coming through. Well, it was such a contrast with Sophia, so warm and lovely."

When the dailies were screened, everyone was relieved, because Heston and Loren together were very powerful and very romantic. The fireworks were there. Rodrigo and Chimene were lighting up the screen, even though on set Heston and Loren were somewhat distant.

Bronston's widow, Dorothea, also told me there were problems with Heston. "He wasn't an easy man to know. He was bristly, sort of, and I think that he was competing with Sophia Loren. And she was charming. One other thing that amused me very much is we were at an opening in London with *El Cid*. The press was waiting downstairs and they had both sort of migrated to the back of the theater. And she got out first. So, of course, the crowd, the press just surrounded her. When he came down, they didn't pay as much attention to him because she'd already gotten press there. He was very miffed about that. He was thinking of himself most of the time."

An added challenge was Bronston's habit of entertaining his international distributors by inviting them to the studio while scenes were being shot. During the first love scene in the film, the studio was filled with 38 distributors watching the intimate scene take place. It couldn't have been fun for Heston or Loren, but served Bronston's campaign to impress his investors and make them feel part of the filmmaking process.

The production was massive, with a literal cast of thousands (mostly the Spanish Army and hundreds more from the Spanish Mounted Police).

Interiors were shot at Madrid's three biggest studios - Chamartin, Sevilla and Cea. There was additional shooting in Rome, mostly done to get the tax breaks that came with an international production. Exteriors used real castles where possible, and new exterior sets (such as the Cathedral at Burgos) where needed.

The Burgos set was one of the largest ever built in Europe. The actual Cathedral at Burgos had been rebuilt many times over the years, and no longer looked medieval, so the Cathedral was reconstructed at the Sevilla studios. The Cathedral took 90 days to build. Because the real Cathedral at Burgos had a stream running through the grounds, the art directors built a channel and flooded it so that the Cathedral set would match the real thing.

A key scene in the film, the fight for Calahorra, was filmed at the nearby Castle Belmonte, which director Anthony Mann found on one of his lengthy location scouts. A difficult and pivotal segment, Rodrigo tests his will and strength in a joust to determine the disputed ownership of the city of Calhorra. The fight itself was directed by Yakima Canutt. The premiere Hollywood stuntman, having worked with Heston in *Ben-Hur,* he had a great reputation as both a stunt creator and director. On *El Cid,* Canutt orchestrated the battles between rival armies, as well as the staging of the broadsword fights. He directed the spectacular fight for Calahorra where Heston fights Don Martin (Christopher Rhodes) that starts as a joust and ends with hand to hand combat. Heston defends himself from a broadsword with a tattered saddle. Heston and British actor Christopher Rhodes trained for a month before any film was ever loaded into the camera. While stuntmen did a lot of the really difficult work, Heston was there for the close-ups and put himself in some jeopardy to make the scene effective. It is, in fact, one of the great scenes of hand to hand combat done for any film.

Heston was trained to handle his weapons by Enzo Musumeci Greco (1910-1994). He trained many actors in swordplay over the years, including Burt Lancaster, Errol Flynn and Steve Reeves. He also worked on the memorable fight with the skeletons in *Jason and the Argonauts* and *The 7th Voyage of Sinbad* for Charles Schneer and Ray Harryhausen. For *El Cid,* Greco worked with Heston and 43 other actors in the film. Heston trained for two months intensively with sword, mace and battle-ax.

The fight itself took five days to film, totaling 31 hours of combat before editing. 70,000 feet of film were shot for the sequence, 34,000 feet were printed, and, when edited down, 1,080 feet remained to make the thrilling 11-minute segment.

Midway through the filming, director Mann decided he should shoot some of the complicated action scenes instead of Canutt. Canutt relates in his book that the two fought loudly over who was best qualified to direct the scenes, with Canutt threatening to leave the picture at one point. Mann came to his senses, and shooting resumed. The results were some of the most spectacular actions scenes ever put on film.

The finale of the film, and the dramatic heart of the story, is the siege and battle for Valencia. Valencia is a modern city today, so the siege was filmed at the coastal city of Pensacola.

Studio publicity proudly pointed out that 348 technicians and laborers reconstructed the walls around the town to mimic 11th-century Valencia. Hundreds of laborers took three months constructing city walls that blocked off modern buildings from the camera. The workers also repaired some of the city's original stone walls. Mann and Canutt used 1,700 trained troops from the Spanish Army, 500 mounted riders from Madrid's Municipal Honor Guard, and every able-bodied man they could find at and around the location. 15 war machines and siege towers were constructed from historical drawings, and 35 boats decorated with battlements became the Moorish fleet. So many local men were recruited that the local fishing fleets stopped working and the orange harvest was delayed.

There is an apocryphal story that one nice sunny day Generalissimo Franco wanted to have a parade of his troops, but was told that they were all away making a Bronston film.

Other statistics were equally awesome: 500 saddles were made for the film, 1,253 pieces of medieval harnesses, 5,780 shields, 40,000 arrows and 800 maces and daggers. These numbing production details give an insight into the scope of the film. Bronston's philosophy was never to rent anything, so costumes, props, and set decorations were all created from scratch. Said Bronston during production, "I want every scene to be real, not just look real."

By any measure, this level of production was lavish according to the producer's son, Bill Bronston. "The film, interestingly enough, used very few sets. They had indoor sets but they found these fabulous castles all over Spain. Their location guy really did a great job for them and those castles were just amazing. With all those assets in Spain, my dad was just thriving in spades. Then Franco gave him the National Cavalry, all those horses and all the army. Part of the deal with the Spanish government was that there had to be a shadow executive staff. Every non-Spanish professional in the upper ranks of the project had to have a paid Spanish counterpart who was nothing but a featherbedded token guy. They hired those people but they didn't do any work. They just got a paycheck."

For the first time in a Bronston film set/costume designers Veniero Colasanti and John Moore worked together, creating historically accurate sets, clothing and set dressings. Colasanti was born in Rome and had designed opera productions as well as some Italian films. Moore was from South Carolina and had been a child prodigy who was producing noteworthy artwork at age seven. The details of the sets are incredible, and are lost unless the film is seen projected on a large screen. Their work on the look of the film was a major undertaking, but by accounts of those who were present during production they enjoyed the work, and spent a not inconsiderable amount of money getting things "right." They scoured museums, studied old tapestries, and consulted with experts to get the costumes and even the small minutiae of the sets correct. A huge debt is owed Colasanti and Moore. Their sets are so detailed that some reviewers thought the interiors were shot on real locations. Every candle-holder, weapon and chair has a proper look of antiquity about it.

Bill Bronston watched them work on his dad's films. "His finding Colasanti and Moore was a quarter of the deal. You had two guys for which money was no object, and when they needed a saddle they built a real saddle. When they needed a sword, they built a real sword. When they needed jewels, they got real jewels, and when they needed furs they got real furs. One of the interesting things was the impact it had on the economy. They really went into high gear in terms of manufacture. So all those swords, all were made in Toledo. In every village, in every direction, there were paid seamstresses bringing in the clothing and the leather. All that was made in Spain, it wasn't made in China, and it wasn't made with special effects. It was all hard, real stuff."

In her autobiography, *The Red and the Blacklist*, Norma Barzman tells of her conversations with Colasanti and Moore: "As we passed the exterior of the studio built exterior of the [Burgos] Cathedral, Moore said, 'Look carefully at the rose window. We got an accomplished artisan, very skilled in painting on glass, to copy it from a Romanesque Church. The Cathedral at Burgos is still standing but it's sixteenth century Gothic. It would have shocked. They built it over the eleventh century Romanesque one in which El Cid and Chimene were actually married. We *had* to build this.' 'We didn't spare anything,' Colasanti said. 'The money was there.'"

As the film took shape, studio publicity cataloged the effort, and the expenditures: 10,000 costumes were created for the film, 700 of brocades and velvet made by the Italian firm of Peruzzi and Carratilli. As Bill Bronston has noted, 2,000 costumes were farmed out to the female population of three cities near Madrid. The Garrido Brothers Foundry of Toledo made battle axes, broadswords and scimitars. $40,000 was spent on jewelry and scepters,

$150,000 for reproduction of medieval art, candelabras, and tapestries.

Samuel Bronston wanted it all to look real. Money was no object. The money flowed, and was spent as fast as the checks could be written.

Bill Bronston wonders what happened to the props after the film was completed. "One of the interesting things is what happened to it? What happened to all that stuff? That's not easy stuff to come apart. Those helmets, shields, armor, saddles, all that clothing, all was in warehouses, and it all totally disappeared. When I went back there, maybe 20 years later, to try and see what was left, and there was nothing. And nobody knew anything. It just vanished."

Colasanti and Moore would return for *55 Days at Peking* and *The Fall of the Roman Empire,* both triumphs of set and costume design.

One of the most memorable parts of *El Cid* is the music. Composed by the great Miklos Rozsa, the score literally explodes off the screen, with both a proper feeling of antiquity and epic grandeur. It is among Rozsa's greatest accomplishments, in a career of great and unprecedented accomplishments.

After a successful score for *King of Kings*, Bronston wanted to be sure he had Rozsa again, even though the composer was scheduled for MGM's epic *Mutiny on the Bounty*. "My first and only thought was Miklos Rozsa. His superb music for such films as *King of Kings* and *Ben-Hur* assured him superiority in Roman Empire music. Did I dare offer him something some 11 centuries later? I made the offer and Dr. Rozsa accepted eagerly after viewing the first rushes."

Basing some of the music on ancient Spanish Cantigas, and spending many weeks researching the music of the period, Rozsa weaves a rich tapestry of authentic-sounding music that adds much to the atmosphere of the film. Some of the incidental and palace music is drawn from thousand-year-old sources, and his music for the fight for Calahorra is some of the most exhilarating music to grace any film. In his autobiography, *A Double Life,* Rozsa wrote: "I spent a month in intense study of the music of the period. I also studied the Spanish folksongs which [Felipe] Pedrell had gone about collecting in the early years of this century. With these two widely differing sources to draw upon, I was ready to compose the music. As always, I attempted to absorb these raw materials and translate them into my own musical language."

The final result was not always to Rozsa's liking. When the film was edited and screened, Rozsa was unhappy. "Again and again," Rozsa wrote, "the sound effects expert [Verna Fields, later film editor for Steven Spielberg's *Jaws*] tried to persuade the director to take out music that interfered with her precious clicks and booms …. At the premier a nasty shock awaited me; scene after scene was music-less. In one scene, the music stopped in mid bar, presumably so the clinking of a sword could be better heard. I was so angry I cancelled a publicity tour I had agreed to undertake; I could not talk about music which nobody was going to hear."

Regardless of his reservations, Rozsa created one of the great film scores of all time. When heard with the film, or on its own, it is a magnificent creation. The music is still performed by orchestras and concert bands today, and the original soundtrack and more up-to-date digitally-recorded performances are solid sellers. Sadly, the original master tapes have been lost, and much of the score that Rozsa wrote for *El Cid* is lost. The tapes that survive have the dreaded sound effects already in them, so unless the score is reconstructed, much of the Rozsa score will never be heard.

The actors, of course, do their jobs well. Besides Heston, who became and remained the quintessential epic hero, and Loren, there is an international cast of British, Italian and French actors that impart dignity and drama to their roles.

French actress Genevieve Page (*Song Without End, Grand Prix, Private Life of Sherlock Holmes*) as Princess Urraca does a fine job in a sinister role, and Raf Vallone (*The Italian Job, The Kremlin Letter, The Other Side of Midnight*), usually playing sinister types, winds up loyal to the Cid and is tortured for him.

The Critics

El Cid was generally highly regarded at the time of its release, and during the brief 1993 re-release of the restored version.

From *Variety* in 1961: "*El Cid* is a fast-action color-rich, corpse-strewn, battle picture. The Spanish scenery is magnificent, the costumes are vivid, the chain mail and Toledo steel gear impressive. Perhaps the 11th century of art directors Veniero Colasanti and John Moore exceeds reality, but only scholars will complain of that. Action rather than acting characterizes this film.

"Yet the film creates respect for its sheer picture making skills. Director Anthony Mann, with assists from associate producer Michael Waszynski who worked closely with him, battle manager Yakima Canutt, and a vast number of technicians, have labored to create stunning panoramic images."

The New York Times (Bosley Crowther) said it "was hard to remember a picture in which the sheer pictorial punch was greater."

Phillip Scheur of the *Los Angeles Times* said, "*El Cid* brings back all the excitement of movie-making, may even bring back the excitement of movie going."

England's *News of the World* said *El Cid* was "certainly one of the year's great pictures."

The Washington Post (reissue review from 1993): "Director Anthony Mann envisioned the story (which had previously inspired operas and plays) as a motion tapestry - an ambition recognized in this version, which, like *Lawrence of Arabia* a few years back, revitalizes *El Cid's* striking visuals and the sweeping score by Miklos Rozsa.

"*El Cid* is a film in which things happen either very quickly or very slowly, but always grandly—the costumes are lavishly colorful, the sets spectacular, the crowds huge, the passions extreme."

The *Austin Chronicle*: (reissue review): "In *El Cid*, Mann took the very medieval pageantry - the castles, the banners, the knights, the Moors - and used them as a landscape; narrow-focusing his cameras on some human dramas (most pitched a bit too hysterically). This historical struggle between the Moors and the Christians for Spain, in Mann's hands becomes a metaphor for freedom fighting, damn the contradictions. A surprisingly effective adventure, *El Cid* begins well enough but if you stick with the story 'til the end, in CinemaScope, it becomes breathtaking."

To add its accolades, *El Cid* was on the 10 best films list of the *New York Times*, the *New York Daily Mirror*, the *Associated Press*, the *Detroit Free Press*, The *Los Angeles Times*, The *Miami Daily News*, the *Boston Globe*, the *Dallas News* and the *Denver Post*.

"Out of the Gates of History into Legend"

So what accounts for the "magic" in *El Cid*? First, it is the thread of historicity to the film, the feeling that the names and the characters are largely real; we're seeing real people existing in what appears to be a real time. In no small way this is because of the contributions of the Barzman screenplay. It is not easy to have actors speak in a way that is historical but does not sound stilted to us today. It is a problem for all epic films, and some succeed at getting the "language" right, but many fail.

Bill Bronston had a theory on why *El Cid* works so well, what the "magic" is. "There was always a very serious preoccupation with striving for authenticity. They really did reach for authenticity and reliability, and they spared no expense to find people who were really authorities. They had the top El Cid authority in the world [Pidal] working on the film. They really submerged themselves in the culture of those films. Those films were all encompassing cultural exercises. When you stop to think about what it takes from a phenomenological standpoint, you're surrounded with a story, you're totally submerged in trying to figure out how to bring that to life at a very intimate level. It's not just walking by a painting.

"Everybody's dressed up. Everybody's speaking in an idiom that reflects the period, and all of a sudden you're transported, into a scenario that you don't know whether it's real or phony. You're living it while you're shooting it. And the reality is what you decide to shoot and there has to be some corrections made as you go along to allow the drama to be psychologically acceptable to the principles that are defining the art, that are making the project. It's not like shooting a mystery movie, where there is no identity loss; they're just sort of people. You're really putting yourself back in time and back into a set of constraints and magical solutions."

Norma Barzman agrees. For her husband, who crafted the screenplay, it *was* magic. "It's mythic. It feels mythic and you can go along with it. You can almost do anything. It's lyric, it's mythic. I think Ben was at his best. I think Ben was so happy to, I think Ben just went into legend too. He was so … it was a moment – not only did he love Sophia, the circumstances were so wonderful – the whole thing was mythic. Just our going to Spain, where we were on a list of people who couldn't come into Spain [because of the blacklist]. With [General Francisco] Franco there and Bronston had arranged it so we were taken in and welcomed. It was crazy. Something about it all, it was like fairyland."

El Cid can't be separated from the time of its creation. John F. Kennedy was President, the world was optimistic about the promise of this new, young administration. Kennedy saw Americans as people who reached out to the world, so the Peace Corps was born, along with a lot of popular initiatives that were noticed around the world. Kennedy himself liked the film, showing it at least three times at the White House. When Charlton Heston was invited to the White House, he was surprised that the President knew about the history of the Cid.

In many respects, *El Cid* was like nothing that came before it and there has been nothing like it since. Like the proverbial perfect storm, all the elements aligned to make a picture that still lives on in the memory of all who have seen it. It is amazing to talk to people who saw it in 1961 and still remember details and whole scenes as if they had seen it just days before. It was created with love and devotion to the art of motion pictures. This is not a film about mundane people having mundane thoughts. Everything about it was epic in proportion. It dealt with great men and great ideas that helped build a nation with honor and trust and devotion to a cause. It speaks to us today as it did to 1960s audiences because these themes are so universal, and perhaps today, it stands as a rarity in an entertainment landscape filled with car chases and superheroes.

El Cid was a struggle to create. Bronston and his team overcame great financial and productions odds and made an epic people compare with *Ben-Hur* and *Lawrence of Arabia*. That he did it in his own unconventional way, without big Hollywood studio interference or money, makes it all the more unique. In *El Cid*, like no other film he produced, the results were artistically pure and financially successful.

The beauty and power of the film are perhaps best summed up at the end. The Cid, dead and lashed to his horse, his lance tied to his hand, rides out to a burst of Rozsa organ music with the sun glinting off his shield. As he rides through hordes of invading Moors, who did not expect to see him again, the music swells with a wordless chorus as the Cid, the horizon and the sky meet at the vanishing point. It is a sublime moment, and it puts a transcendent finishing touch on one of the great epics in motion picture history.

55 Days at Peking

"A handul of men and women held
out against bloodthirsty fanatics."

Released in 1963. **Original screenplay**: Philip Yordan and Bernard Gordon; **Director**: Nicholas Ray; **Second Unit Director**: Andrew Marton; **Music**: Dimitri Tiomkin; **Producer**: Samuel Bronston and distributed by Allied Artists; **Running time**: 150 minutes; **Cast**: Charlton Heston, Ava Gardner, David Niven, Elizabeth Sellars, Flora Robson, John Ireland, Robert Helpmann, Leo Genn, Kurt Kasznar, Harry Andrews, Lynne Sue Moon, Paul Lukas, Jerome Thor.

5 Days at Peking was supposed to be the fourth major film produced by Bronston in Spain. It became the third when Charlton Heston balked at doing *The Fall of the Roman Empire,* but was intrigued by the story of the 1900 Boxer Rebellion in China.

In a way, the film is stuck in the era in which it was produced. Today it would not be seen to be very politically correct as it deals with a heroic effort of members of several countries' foreign legations inside Peking to hold off a siege by the Boxers (radical Chinese terrorists intent on driving the Europeans and Americans out of China).

The film was said to be the last movie President Kennedy saw before he was assassinated in Dallas in November of 1963. Kennedy was a fan of *El Cid*, and seemed to like the spectacle and heroism of the Bronston films. Of course, the themes of *El Cid* and *55 Days at Peking*, along with many of the other Bronston films, reflected many of Kennedy's own dreams and view of the world.

Like all Bronston films, the production values are very high, and the depiction of the Forbidden City, the legations, and surrounding buildings are first rate. At the time of release, the Peking set was the largest ever built for a motion picture. (Bronston surpassed himself when he filmed *The Fall of the Roman Empire*, his next production.) Sets and costumes are up to Bronston's usual high standards, and this was another triumph for Veniero Colasanti and John Moore. This was director Nicholas Ray's second film for Bronston, the first being *King of Kings*. Ray was taken ill on the set, and was essentially fired by Bronston and replaced by Guy Green (*Diamond Head*) at the request of Charlton Heston and then Green was replaced by Andrew Marton, the second unit director on the film. Marton was most famous for directing the chariot race in *Ben-Hur*. Neither Green nor Marton was credited as director. Some additional scenes were directed by Noel Howard, who was listed as Second Unit Director.

Budgeted at 17 million dollars, the film grossed only five million in the United States, although it made money overseas. For Bronston, the film was a disappointment coming off the massive success of *El Cid*. Like *El Cid*, U.S. distribution was by Allied Artists.

From the start, *55 Days* was a troubled production, with clashes between the writers and the stars, the director and Bronston, and difficulties with a script that was literally being written as the movie was being made. Bernard Gordon, the key writer of the film, has little good to say about it, and told me, "I just thought it was a trashy picture: a big, splashy, nothing picture with cardboard characters. It was not my idea of great filmmaking. I didn't think MGM and [William] Wyler [*Ben-Hur*] would have made that picture."

It was one of a series of what might be called "siege pictures," which were in vogue at the time, along with *The Alamo*, *Khartoum*, *Zulu*, and, to some degree, elements of Bronston's own *King of Kings* and *El Cid*.

The Story

China in 1900 is over-run with foreigners. The film opens with impressive crane shots of the various foreign legations raising their flags in the morning as the camera moves back between them their national anthems blend into a cacophony of brass instruments.

A squadron of Marines led by Charlton Heston arrives at the foreign compound, but stops to bargain unsuccessfully for the life of a priest who is being tortured by Chinese peasants.

The Dowager Empress of China, Tzu-Hsi (Flora Robson), is troubled by all the foreigners who have come to China to trade. She worries that extended trade will lead to occupation. Her two main advisors are split, with Prince Tuan (Robert Helpmann) considering the Europeans "devils" and General Jung-Lu (Leo Genn) more liberal. The general is more worried about the fanatical Boxers, who are running amok in the country and killing missionaries and other foreigners. He is losing favor because the Empress supports the Boxers in their zeal to rid the country of the western elements.

As the threats continue to pile up, the Europeans, led by Britain's Sir Arthur Robertson (David Niven), devise plans to defend themselves if the Boxers over-run the legations. Major Matt Lewis (Charlton Heston) commands a brigade of U.S. Marines and he is apolitical, but sees he is being asked to do a job, and like any good Marine, executes his mission. There is a romantic sub-plot in the film as Baroness Natalie Ivonoff (Ava Gardner) finds herself attracted to Major Lewis and they have a brief love affair as a dozen countries band together to defend themselves against the Boxer siege.

The countries hold off the invading Boxers, who use everything from rockets to siege towers, for 55 days (hence the film's title) until relief comes from a multinational force as the Empress leaves Peking disguised as a peasant.

The History

After Japan defeated China in 1895, European countries began a process they called "carving up the melon." With China in a state of weakness, strategic parts of China fell under the influence of European states.

The British took the territories around Hong Kong while the Russians took Port Arthur. In addition, Germany took land near Shantung. The United States showed little interest in China initially, and was concentrating on exercising power in Guam and the Philippines. Because of the United States failure to gain a foothold in China, it actively supported an "open door" policy to make sure it was not shut off from trade or other influence.

China was, of course, not happy watching its territories being carved up, and many clandestine groups began to form to keep China out of the hands of its rivals. One of the strongest of these was called the "Righteous and Harmonious Fists," which the Europeans called the Boxers, due to their marching with their fists clenched the way a boxer's fists are made.

Originally, these secret sects were considered a threat to the Imperial Government, and were suppressed or ignored, but as outside elements gained strength in China, the rulers realized these militant groups could be used to drive out the foreigners. The politics of the situation is well presented in the film. Most historians don't characterize the Boxer Rebellion as either a rebellion, or a war, but the Boxers were putting continuous pressure on the European interests who were exercising more and more influence in China.

Most of the regional Governors of the provinces were more interested in preserving the peace than seeing violent revolution against the foreigners. Still and all, more than 230 foreigners were killed, along with thousands of Chinese Christians.

The Dowager Empress had her imperial troops join the boxers, who laid siege to the foreign legation beginning on June 20, 1900. The legation included personnel and families from the United Kingdom, Belgium, the Netherlands, Russia, Germany, the United States and Japan. As in the movie, these legations were all located in the same block, and they banded together to hold off the Chinese forces.

The provocations of the Boxers did not work, and on August 14, 1900 an international force of 20,000 stormed into Beijing (then called Peking) and essentially rescued the besieged Europeans and put the Chinese Government under virtual house arrest.

This led to the establishment of the "Boxer Protocol," putting the Chinese government under severe economic sanctions, opening Peking to the presence of foreign military troops, and it led to the prosecution of those government officials who had collaborated with the Boxers.

How accurate is the film as history? The screenplay does try to tell the story from both sides, but clearly the heroes are those that inhabit the foreign legation to hold out from the siege of the Boxers. The general outline of the story is fairly accurate, and many of the characters are based on real people even though their names are changed. The head of the British legation was Claude Mac-Donald, not Arthur Robertson. The Charlton Heston character is made up, but provides dramatic tension. Flora Robson does a good job portraying the Dowager Empress, Hzu Tsi, and in fact looks remarkably like photos of the real Hzu Tsi. The blowing up of the Chinese armory and the dramatic attack of the Boxers using siege towers are inventions of the filmmakers.

The Production

The film is another dazzling display of cinematography and art direction somewhat weighed down with a jingoistic plot and a muddled storyline. To their credit, the filmmakers try to take a neutral stand on the politics of the incident, giving time to the Chinese point of view, as well as the westerners, but at times the film becomes just a standard action film. In today's world, it is hard to identify with the imperialist west, and easy to sympathize with the Chinese who are trying to fend off threats to their culture and economy.

For director Nicholas Ray, it was a return to the epic form (*King of Kings* was his first Bronston epic) and Ray's use of the widescreen Super Technirama frame is appropriate and sometimes stirring.

The origin of the film story came from principal writer, Bernard Gordon, who told me it came up in a conversation with Philip Yordan. "I was under contract to Yordan at the time. We were living and working in Paris. At one point he said to me, 'I need a big picture. You know, films are changing these days. They have television. Now they can see pictures for nothing and you've got to get them into the theaters with something big and splashy. Big productions. Big titles.' And he would nag me day after day: 'come up with it; come up with an idea for another picture for Bronston.' And I would come up with a sheet of titles. One of them that I came up with was The Boxer Rebellion, because when I had been in the Story Department at Paramount I had the job of finding projects for the producers from old unproduced or produced pictures and films and stories that they had in files, 16,000 of them. One of them was a story that intrigued me at the time – this is long before I knew any of these people – was about the Boxer Rebellion. It was a play. And unfortunately I had lost the book which I had prepared for this – I had given it to a producer and never got it back – and that particular play was in there. But anyway I remembered the Boxer Rebellion as an interesting subject for a picture, which I proposed to Yordan. He said, 'No, no, no. Whoever heard of the Boxer Rebellion? How do you sell a picture called The Boxer Rebellion? Forget it.'

"Yordan always made a habit of going into a bookstore and looking at all the titles on the shelves. What he was looking for was a title that would strike him as being a good idea. He didn't care about the story, but a good title, something you could sell. He pulled out this book and there was a chapter in it, *55 Days at Peking*, and he said that's it! And he came back to Paris and he said, 'I got the thing I want to do.' I said, 'For Christssake, I gave that to you.' He said, 'No, no, no. What you said had nothing to do with it.' Well, what the hell, I was being paid. What could I do? So it became *55 Days at Peking*. It was very difficult because none of us knew anything about the Boxer Rebellion and I had very little access to any kind of research there in Madrid. We had no story, we had no characters, we had nothing. Just blank pages, you know. So I was set to work writing, and I did work with Yordan who was not good at story but was very good at promotional materials, scenes. He was a showman."

The reconstruction of Peking, which included the headquarters of 12 countries in the foreign compound and the imperial palace, was spectacular. In the end, not much of those sets were seen.

Bernard Gordon felt the shooting of the picture was so disorganized that his script was never designed properly to utilize the sets. "He [Nicholas Ray] knew how to make good scenes of people together, talking together. But he didn't know how to do big epics. For example, when the picture made rough cut and I went to see it, I said to the film editor who was an old friend of mine, 'There isn't one shot of that big wall that cost three-quarters of a million dollars. Where is it?' And Bobby [film editor Robert Lawrence] said to me, 'Come here, I'll show you where it is.' He pulled out about this much of the film and said, 'This was done, shot before the picture . . . And that's all I ever had? What can I do with that?' Well, Nick didn't understand, that shouldn't be that way, you know. So he was very unsure of himself."

Gordon worried that sets had been built without a workable screenplay. Clearly, they were doing things the wrong way round. "When I first saw the mockup of the set, I was appalled. I said, 'Listen, Nick, I wrote the script and I have certain battle scenes described in detail, and I don't know where you are going to put the camera to get any of it.' He said, 'Don't worry, don't worry, Bernie, I know what I'm doing.' As a matter of fact, they hired an Italian cameraman [Aldo Tonti]. He came and looked at the script and looked at the set, and he just walked out! He just couldn't do it." [Gordon quoted in *Nicholas Ray* by Bernard Eisenschitz]

On top of that, while the sets were spectacular, Gordon feels far too much money was spent on things that were never seen. He was especially critical when real gold leaf was used on the furniture and trim of the imperial palace set by art directors Colasanti and Moore. "As if it makes any difference on the film whether it's gold leaf or just gold paint," Gordon told me, "on a chair, which you may or may not see in the picture. But when the production manager came to me and said, 'It's crazy. They're throwing so much money away. It's costing a fortune to put gold leaf on. It's got to be done a sheet at a time. Why don't you do something?' I said, 'What do you want me to do? I'm just a lousy writer on this thing. You're the Production Manager. Go talk to Bronston.' So he did. He went across the hall and talked to Bronston and Bronston said, 'I want it to be the best of everything.' That's all he knew. Should be the best. But money was thrown away that way, because Colasanti and Moore probably had in mind that they would take these things back to Rome with them, which they probably did."

Even worse, the intricate carvings done in the imperial palace were done on black walls. They simply did not show up on camera, so all the work and the money it took to make them was wasted.

They also used real silk for gowns instead of imitation silk, even though the imitation variety showed up better on camera. It was part of the Bronston mantra of "make it real." Actually, some of the costumes *were* real. They were loaned to the production by a family that wanted to stay anonymous. The costumes were actually from Tzu-His's court. Some of the principals wore them, including Flora Robson and Robert Helpmann.

To call the film a "troubled production" would be a massive understatement. As always, the production was short on petty cash, and the crew was not always sure their next paycheck would arrive on time. While Bronston was busy wooing potential distributors and showing off the sets, the film was getting further and further behind schedule. As Bronston's assistants tried to move things along, director Ray was getting more and more frustrated.

Bronston was switching out executives and finally Michael Wasynski was made Vice President of Production after Jamie Prades was eased out. Clearly, no one was watching the expenditures. According to Bernard Eisenschitz's biography of Ray, "Theft was rife at every level of the organization. Editing tables, typewriters, sets of stills disappeared." John Melson, a writer from Yordan's group, was quoted as saying, "Anyone at all could go to the concierge at the Hilton lobby and say, 'Would you give me an airplane ticket to Paris and charge it to the Bronston organization?'"

As Bernard Gordon said, the sets were overbuilt. And largely unseen. In Charlton Heston's diaries, he notes that two thirds of the sets were never utilized in the film, and he implored Bronston in vain to let Orson Welles come in and shoot a quick thriller.

Meanwhile, Alan Brown, the film's associate producer, said, "Some of Sam's loyal lieutenants were departing for Zurich regularly with suitcases, and coming back the same day without suitcases. Sam, apparently, didn't get any of that money." [Eisenschitz]

Bernard Gordon also said Bronston should have had better people around him. "But Sam liked to be surrounded by people he'd known a long time and trusted, and felt comfortable with. He did really strange things, but most of what I know about Bronston is what I got from Yordan secondhand. I mean, for example, one day I'm walking down the street with Yordan and he says, 'Goddamn Bronston, he's paying 10% a month on a lousy little $10,000 or $20,000 he owes some crooks in Rome.' And I say to Sam, 'Why don't you just pay it off?' And Sam said, 'Well, I need the cash,' so he kept paying 10% a month, it didn't matter to him. That kind of thing, which I think must have been true. I don't think Yordan was inventing anything like that."

Nicholas Ray was having his own problems. According to Gordon, a big epic was just too far away from the kind of intimate, character-driven pictures Ray excelled at making. "Oh, Nick Ray. Well, I can talk to you about Nick Ray because I liked him very much until it turned out he was a weakling in relation to making decisions. He was totally out of his mold in that big picture. He didn't know what the hell he was doing. He knew how to make good scenes of people together, talking together. But he didn't know how to do big scenes."

There is still controversy over what went wrong and why Ray was forced out. One reason was that the film was taking too long to produce, and Bronston had already committed to a release date and was well along with pre-production planning on *The Fall of the Roman Empire*. He had also promised a delivery date for that film as well, and the delays on *55 Days* were making it clear the schedule would be compromised.

Ray seemed to be straining at getting the days' shooting schedule completed, and complained that he did not have enough help. Many of the Bronston team was tied up on *The Fall of the Roman Empire*, and the schedule fell further behind. Heston and others could see Ray was not dealing well with the strain.

Then Ray got sick, perhaps it was the pressure of the shooting schedule, or pressure from Bronston's assistants, or pressure from the demanding cast. It was thought originally to be a heart attack, but it turned out not to be so serious, and after a few weeks Ray signaled that he was ready to come back to work. But Yordan, speaking for Bronston, fired him, and some scenes were shot by Guy Green, who was recommended by Heston. Then Andrew Marton was brought in to finish the production, but Marton completely reorganized the structure of some sections of the film, trimming some scenes, removing others, and adding new footage. In the end, almost half the film was directed by Marton, a bit less than half by Ray, and a few minutes by Guy Green.

There was also a shortage of steel tubing in Spain that was needed to support the set, and it was determined that *55 Days* had to be finished and the set struck so that the Roman Forum could be built in its place using the same steel. When Marton arrived, the picture was in a sorry state, and he was given the instruction to finish the picture, and finish it quickly.

Tadeo Villalba, a Bronston production manager, said when Marton took over for Ray, things happened very fast. "Marton swept into the set like Attila the Hun. You should have seen that set. We were all frightened because each day it was being bombarded in such a way that it could never be used again, burning on all sides. Marton had received strict orders from Bronston to complete the film in two weeks; we felt as though we were in the authentic battle of Peking. It was incredible." Then, when the film was done, Villalba said, "Without wasting a day, the old tubing was rushed over the build the new sets; Roman temples went up all over the place. If more tubing had been available, the sets would have been even bigger." [Quoted in *Behind the Spanish Lens* by Peter Besas]

Marton felt he had inherited a mess. In an oral history interview with Joanne D'Antonio, Marton talked about how he quickly created a new beginning and ending for the film. "When I came on board I thought the picture was very shallow, just action, action, action - there was no meaning. I wrote a new beginning and a new ending and submitted them to management - who consisted of Bronston and Michael Waszynski. Waszynski was an agent originally - not really a hands-on film person. Anyway, they said 'No' with a capital N capital O. And I was very unhappy."

About that time, John Ford visited the set and encouraged Marton to shoot his new scenes anyway, so Marton scheduled a crew and extras and did it without management noticing.

Marton said, "After it was shot, the management said, 'you were not supposed to shoot - we can't use it.' I said, 'Why not ask the film editor to put it in there and see what it looks like.'

"Well, it went into the film, and it was never moved again. It was left in, in the same spot - at the opening of the picture. It gave the whole story a deeper meaning. You go from embassy to embassy - they're playing their national anthem, all on top of each other. We showed the American flag going up, and the camera moves over all of Peking and end up on a little Chinese chow house where two old Chinese are eating. Hearing all this cacophony of national anthems, one says to the other, 'What is this terrible noise?' And the other one says 'Different nations saying the same thing at the same time: We want China.' And that was the opening of the picture." [From the *Director's Guild Oral History*, published 1991]

Marton works a similar scene for the end, as the western armies come together each playing their own march with a jumble of noise that mirrors the opening of the picture. Charlton Heston hears it and says, "For 55 days we played the same tune … maybe people will remember some day."

Marton's efforts on the film contributed to a tightening and strengthening of the drama, and made the film more coherent.

Music for the film was by Academy Award-winning composer Dimitri Tiomkin (*High Noon, The Alamo, Gunfight at the O.K. Corral*). Tiomkin, known for his flamboyant behavior and showy music, delivered a score that was loud and eccentric. Sometimes Oriental-sounding, sometimes more action-oriented like his *Guns of Navarone* score, the music is anything but subtle. As in many Tiomkin scores, *55 Days at Peking* contains a song, "So Little Time," sung by Andy Williams, to try and get some radio play and free promotion. The song and the score were nominated for Oscars, but neither won. While the film score is OK, Tiomkin went on to write a major opus for *The Fall of the Roman Empire* that was both popularly and critically praised.

Casting

The film starred Charlton Heston, Ava Gardner, David Niven and

Paul Lukas. Heston liked the idea of the film because he got to play in a historical drama about a real event (like *El Cid* and not at all like *Ben-Hur*, which was based on a novel). Heston liked to be involved at all levels of the film's production, and script author Bernard Gordon was not wild about Heston.

"Well, I didn't like Heston, I didn't like his politics, and I like him even less now. I've been on the air with him and so on but the National Rifle Association stuff is not my kind of thing. But, see, I never went onto sets and see how the work, what was happening on the sets. I was too busy up in my room writing all the time. Sometimes on three or four scripts at the same time. Anyway, they have no respect for writers, you know. Actors and directors are not inclined to work with writers, because if you work with a writer on the set you're in trouble. He says why did you do it that way? That's not what I wrote. That's not what it should be. And so on. So writers are generally kept off. And I was kept off and I wasn't a good self-promoter in the way that some other writers are, working with directors and producers."

David Niven was also engaged by Bronston, and that led to more problems for Gordon. "He [Bronston] met David Niven in a hotel in Rome and said, 'Hey, David, want to do a picture for me? I'll give you $300,000,' which was a lot of money at that time. And Niven said yeah, and they had a deal. But Niven hadn't seen anything on paper and wound up having major problems with the script."

Niven felt he did not have very much to do, and didn't seem to be a strong character in the film, just sort of a pal of Heston's character. Gordon was called in out of a vacation to write a strong scene for Niven and the actress who played his wife, Elizabeth Sellars. Gordon called it a "hamlet scene," because it gave Niven a strong emotional scene to play.

Continued on page 118

Sam Bronston in Hollywood in the 40's.

Before Bronston went to Spain, he spent a few years in Hollywood as a Producer. One his his best known films there was the excellent *A Walk in the Sun* with Lloyd Bridges, Dana Andrews and Richard Conte made in 1945. Difficulties with the studio surrounding financing eventually led to Bronston's name being taken off the picture.

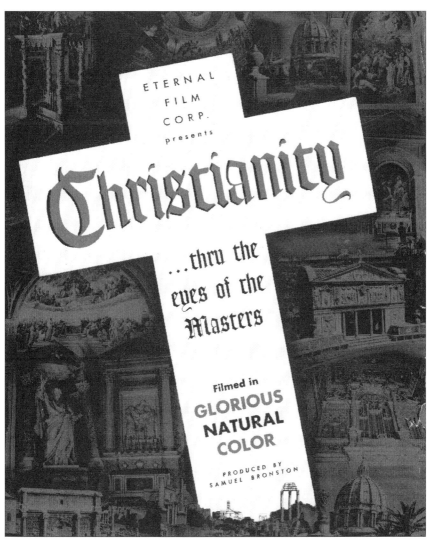

A poster for Bronston's 1951 Documentary *Mosaics-Pictures for Eternity* done for the Vatican.

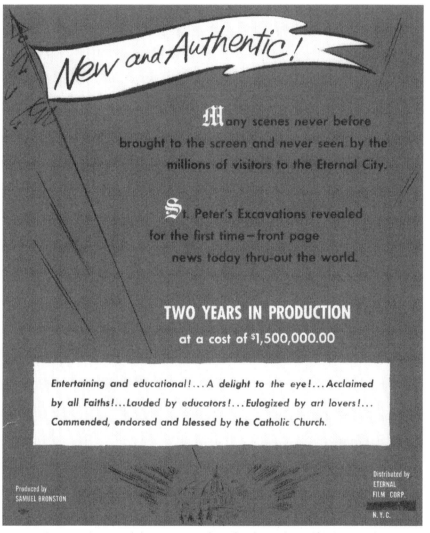

New and Authentic!

Many scenes never before brought to the screen and never seen by the millions of visitors to the Eternal City.

St. Peter's Excavations revealed for the first time – front page news today thru-out the world.

TWO YEARS IN PRODUCTION
at a cost of $1,500,000.00

Entertaining and educational!...A delight to the eye!...Acclaimed by all Faiths!...Lauded by educators!...Eulogized by art lovers!... Commended, endorsed and blessed by the Catholic Church.

Produced by
SAMUEL BRONSTON

Distributed by
ETERNAL
FILM CORP.

N. Y. C.

Bronston's second documentary done for the Vatican- The St. Peter's Excavations, a 1951 film that helped cement Bronston's relationship with the Pope. That relationship led to his getting script approval for *King of Kings*.

The Patriots come ashore in a scene from Bronston's *John Paul Jones*.

Ships outfitted to match the period cruise off the Spanish coastline for *John Paul Jones*.

Robert Stack goes over his lines while aboard ship
during the filming of *John Paul Jones*.

Bronson, as always in a coat and tie, during the filming of the
Sermon on the Mount sequence for *King of Kings*.

Bronston watches preparations for the Sermon on the Mount scene in
King of Kings. Jamie Prades, Associate Producer
is to Bronston's right in the foreground.

Bronston (left) with
Associate Producer
Jamie Prades on the
King of Kings set.

Actor Frank Thring (center) plays Herod Antipas in *King of Kings*.
Thring played Pilate in Ben-Hur, and went on to have a role in *El Cid*.

Jeffrey Hunter serves the Last Supper in a creatively staged scene by Director Nicholas Ray in *King of Kings*.

The Shadow of the risen Christ forms a cross on the banks of the
Sea of Galilee in *King of Kings*. As described in the book, Ray
Bradbury had devised another finale for the film which was scrapped.

Charlton Heston
meets Sophia
Loren at the
Madrid Airport
for the beginning
of filming for
El Cid.

Charlton Heston as El Cid, looks over the wounds
of Gary Raymond, playing Prince Sancho.

In a scene from *El Cid* Charlton Heston (left) questions whether his
captives Douglas Wilmer (center) and Frank Thring should be executed.

El Cid's loyal soldiers beg him to come out of exile and resume his fight to unify Spain.

Actress Genevieve Page as Princess Urraca and John Frazer in a scene from *El Cid*.

A production still from *El Cid* with Raf Vollone (left),
Sophia Loren and Charlton Heston.

Bronston (right)
and Associate
Producer Jamie
Prades discuss the
filming of *El Cid*.

Elizabeth Sellars, Robert Helpmann, David Niven,
Charlton Heston and Ava Gardner *in 55 Days at Peking.*

A view of the magnificent set for *55 Days at Peking.*

A Production still showing the Boxer's Seige of the
foreign compound from *55 Days at Peking.*

An aerial view of the *55 Days at Peking* set built at Las Matas near Madrid.
At the time it was the largest set ever built for a film, until it was replaced
on this same site with the forum set for "Fall of the Roman Empire"

Charlton Heston and Ava Gardner in a scene from *55 Days at Peking*.
In truth, the actors did not get along and the set was filled with tension.

A spectacular set built for *Fall of the Roman Empire* representing a northern outpost on
the Roman frontier. The design of the fort is accurate to the period of the film.

A portion of the magnificent Roman forum set built full scale at Las Matas outside Madrid. It is one of the largest sets ever built for a motion picture.

Another view of the forum built for *Fall of the Roman Empire*.
This scene is from the finale, as Empire Commodus' enemies are burned alive.

Bronston on the *Fall of
the Roman Empire* set.

119

Bronston (center) Inspects the *Fall of the Roman Empire* set
with designer John Colasanti (left) and an associate.

Actress Sophia Loren arrives for a day of shooting on *Fall of the Roman Empire*.
Her co-star Stephen Boyd can be seen at the extreme left.

Bronston (left) and Director Anthony
Mann on one of the many sets for *Fall
of the Roman Empire*.

The Circus Maximus capsizes in a spectacular scene from *Circus World*.
How this scene was accomplished is described in the Circus World chapter.

Bronston poses in
his Madrid office

The cast of *Circus World*. Left to right; John Smith,
Claudia Cardinale, John Wayne and Rita Hayworth

"Well, you have to give Yordan credit because I had my only lit-tle vacation trip I took to Monaco, because the doctor at the hotel said to Yordan, 'You've got to give this guy some time off, or he's going to have trouble.' So Yordan says to me, 'What do you want to do?' I said, 'I just want to take a week and go someplace with a beach.' He said, 'Well, what'll you do on the beach?' I said, 'I'll just sit there and enjoy it.' He said, 'Yeah, but what will you do the second day?' His idea of life without a telephone was something unbelievable. Anyway, I went to Monaco and the second day I was there I had a call from him saying that David Niven had gotten a script and said he wasn't going to do a picture. Now, he'd signed and Yordan said, 'I offered to let him out of it. No, he wanted the money.' So Yordan said to me, 'We have to do something.' And I said, 'Well, what the hell can I do now? This picture's being shot. What do I know about how to make him happy?' So Yordan said, 'Give him a Hamlet scene. It always works.' So I was ferried back to Madrid and met with a great, big Cadillac sedan at the airport and driven quickly to my rooms, and I sat down and wrote the Hamlet scene. I thought it was kind of crazy."

Those problems were nothing compared to the issues with Ava Gardner. On her best days, she was considered unstable, and Heston had already voiced misgivings about her casting.

In his autobiography, *In the Arena*, Heston describes an early script meeting Gardner attended. "She seemed very edgy, saying little until her second vodka tonic, when she launched on a diatribe trashing the entire project and just about everything she had to do in it. This may have been Ava's first experience with a full court press script conference; in her time at MGM, actors didn't sit in on script meetings. Nevertheless, she was an instinctive mistress of the slash and burn technique: destroy everything in sight, wait till they sweep away the ashes and rescue the children, then start again."

As production continued, Gardner was late for morning calls, and was increasingly abusive to cast and crew. At one point, a crewmember grabbed a still photo of her and she stormed off the set for the rest of the day.

It was putting increasing stress on Nicholas Ray, who already had all the stress he could handle. Finally, a decision was made to give her a death scene and get her out of the movie.

Bernard Gordon told me there was nothing else they could do. "She was unhappy all the way through the picture. Her whole career was really on the downs, and she was constantly drunk. And she just walked off, that's all. They couldn't locate her so they had to finish without her."

The idea for writing Gardner out of the picture came from Ben Barzman, who had written *El Cid*. His wife Norma told me it was Ben's only contribution to *55 Days at Peking*. "Well, that was Ben's suggestion. Let her be dead. Let them carry out a corpse of her dead, then she doesn't have to act it, and then she's gone. That was all he did. He took a plane from Nice to Madrid and they said, 'What'll we do?' And Ben said, 'Kill her. It's easy. It's so easy to put her on a stretcher.'"

The way the scene was finished in the film, Gardner's character is in a hospital bed, having been wounded during the Boxer siege. Paul Lukas, playing a physician, looks down at her with a sad expression and pulls the sheet over her. Of course, Gardner was already out of the production, and an extra stood in for the deceased character under the sheet.

In his career, Heston has had problems with his leading ladies. In truth, he has had some temperamental co-stars, but there was, especially in his earlier films, a pervasive dislike of female actresses.

In an interview with the *London Daily Express* around the time of

55 Days in Peking, Heston let loose. "By and large, actresses are a different breed of cat. Most of them, I wouldn't touch with a pole - or work with where I have some control over the production. It appalls and disgusts me, the amateur way most of them treat film-making. The rule of thumb for most of those broads is to be 20 minutes late in the morning and 10 minutes late after lunch."

One other aspect of the picture is the 4,000 Chinese extras. Madrid is not the first place you think of to film the battle of Peking, so the Bronston organization had to round up Chinese extras at every restaurant and laundry they could find, first in Spain and then expanding the casting call to Europe. It was said at the time, only half jokingly, that it was impossible to get a Chinese meal in Spain while the movie was being made.

Reviews

Like many of the Bronston films, reviewers praised the sets and costume design, but were not as impressed with the writing or story.

The New York Times, May 30, 1963: "As a fictional version of the final gasps of the dying Manchu Dynasty in and around the Forbidden City in 1000, it is no more historic than a Gene Autry epic. But Nicholas Ray, director; his associate, Andrew Marton; Philip Yordan and Bernard Gordon, the script writers, and an energetic cast have made these '55 Days' rousing, sometimes exciting, action fare that should keep the customers alert and entertained even if their intellects are confused.

"But the film remains in memory for its flashing movement and fireworks. The producers were sensible enough to keep the dialogue, which is often banal, to a minimum.

"Although it was all done in and around Madrid, the sound and fury and beauty of these momentous '55 Days at Peking' are brought vividly to life. Most of the principals and their stories are not."

Variety, January 1963: "While Ray is identified as director, some of the battle scenes actually were directed by Andrew Marton. This came to be in a period when Ray was ill.

"David Niven is the British embassy head who stubbornly refuses to surrender, risking the safety of all about him, including his wife and two children. Both he and Charlton Heston perform with conviction, Heston as the American Marine major who commands the defense. Ava Gardner's role is not too well conceived. Hers is the part of the widow of a Russian bigshot who killed himself upon learning of his wife's infidelity with a Chinese official.

"Jack Hildyard's photography is excellent, particularly in getting on the big screen the savage attack scenes which take up the major part of the picture. Dimitri Tiomkin provides engaging music."

Summing Up

55 Days didn't make a profit in the United States, but recouped its nine-million-dollar investment with pre-bookings in the rest of the world. Bronston felt it was time to move on to his shelved *The Fall of the Roman Empire*, which would be bigger and, he hoped, bring him the notoriety and profits he and his investors expected.

55 Days in Peking came out reasonably well considering the conditions under which it was created. It has spectacle, good performances from Niven, Flora Robson, and Leo Genn. Heston has no on-screen chemistry with Ava Gardner. He did not like working with her, and she was there only because Heston finally gave in to Bronston and his executives and allowed her to be hired. It was a decision Heston came to regret.

Nicholas Ray, a well thought of and talented director, was simply in over his head in another Bronston epic. That the film works as well as it does is due in large part to the complex reworking of the existing footage, and smart decisions on new footage that needed to be undertaken. Andrew Marton brought more coherence to the story and provided a thoughtful opening and closing to the film, that doubtless made it more accessible to audiences.

Like many Bronston films, it is the sets and art direction that stand out. Colasanti and Moore once again worked their magic, sparing no expense to create colossal sets and intricate interiors that dazzle the eye.

The set, at the time, the largest ever constructed for a motion picture, was surely misused, and there were clearly opportunities for better use of both the constructed building, and better camera angles that showcased them, but the multiple changes of directors and speed of the production let those chances slide.

We're left with a good adventure film with a pretty firm grounding in history. In better hands, *55 Days at Peking* could have been a more intelligent exploration of the issues involved, perhaps as good as Heston's *Khartoum* made three years later.

Today, we see the film through more jaundiced eyes, looking more cynically at foreign adventure and cultural domination. It is hard to cheer for the Europeans, the Japanese and the Americans, who are eager to exploit the Chinese and dominate its culture.

For Bronston, it was a painstakingly assembled, uplifting adventure story and another step in his personal quest to make films of importance. Once again, Bronston had created a film with attention to details that left many wondering how such an elaborate film could be produced so quickly.

Seen as a film of its time, it is fondly remembered by many for what it was, and what it might have been.

The Fall of the Roman Empire

"The Most Magnificcent Recration
of an Ancient Empire."

Screenplay: Ben Barzman, Basilio Franchina and Philip Yordan; **Director**: Anthony Mann; **Producer**: Samuel Bronston. **Cast**: Sophia Loren, Stephen Boyd, Alec Guinness, James Mason, Christopher Plummer, Anthony Quayle, John Ireland, Mel Ferrer, Omar Sharif; **Released**: Paramount Pictures. Shot in Ultra Panavision 70 (Aspect Ratio 2.35:1 in 35mm prints) **Running time**: 188 minutes.

The ironies abound in this beautifully crafted but uneven 20-million-dollar film.

The Fall of the Roman Empire was also the beginning of the fall of the Bronston empire. After losing 18 million dollars, Bronston was able to produce one more film, *Circus World*, but the financial death spiral was not reversible.

If you saw *Gladiator* (2000), directed by Ridley Scott, you saw essentially a remake of *The Fall of the Roman Empire*. The time period the films are set in is the same, the characters are essentially the same, and the plot follows the same outline. I think the Bronston/ Anthony Mann version is the better movie.

Charlton Heston was asked to star in this film, but did not like the early version of the script and passed. Kirk Douglas was courted, but he passed as well. So did Richard Harris, who was asked to play Commodus. (Forty years later Harris would play Marcus Aurelius in *Gladiator*.)

Stephen Boyd got the Heston part, and at least in this film was able to win a chariot race, not lose, as he did in *Ben-Hur*.

A further irony is that this film contained almost the same exact production staff as the highly successful *El Cid*, so it seemed to have the right people on board. It had the same director (Anthony Mann), the same writer (Ben Barzman), the same set and costume designers (Venerio Colasanti and John Moore), the same cinematographer (Robert Krasker) and the editing skills of Robert Lawrence. It also had Sophia Loren, who was such a big part of the success of *El Cid*.

Will Durant, an expert on Rome and its ancient history, was brought on as consultant and the film's opening and closing narrations quote from his seminal book, *Caesar and Christ*. Durant decided on what time period the film would center, and what the major issues were in the empire's decline.

"Out of a hundred factors in the decline and fall of Rome," said Durant, "our picture chooses two: The pressure of the barbarians upon the frontiers, and the tragic reign of the half-insane Commodus. In the year 180 the ailing father and the presumptive, presumptuous son were leading Roman legions against Germanic tribes along the Danube between Singidunun, which is now Belgrade, and Vindobonum, which became Vienna."

The technical work was stunning, and *Fall* had the largest set ever built for a movie to date, a 3-dimensional recreation of the Roman Forum measuring more than a thousand feet long. Populated by thousands of accurately dressed extras, it was an amazing site to behold. Will Durant was dazzled by the forum set, and said he believed the buildings were faithful reproductions "as far as scholarship can recall them."

The film purports to explain the fall of Rome, but that is a bit much for any drama to take on. Rome fell for hundreds of years, and even a lengthy motion picture would have its work cut out for it. What happened to Rome over 300 or 400 years is not easily told, even in a three-hour movie. It took Edward Gibbon 6 volumes in his *Decline and Fall of the Roman Empire*.

But *Fall* does capture the mood. Will Durant spoke of the empire undergoing a "cultural and spiritual fatigue," and it is visible throughout. The first portion of the film, lasting 75 minutes, from the opening images to the death of Marcus Aurelius, is almost *film noir*. Shot in the Sierra Guadarrama in Spain, there are endless cloudiness, snow, and darkness. Rooms are lit by candle glow; conspiracies are born in dark corners. This first part depicts the last days of Emperor Aurelius in a reflective mood as death approaches. For accuracy, some of the dialog comes from his own written *Meditations*. The second part of the film, by contrast, takes place in sunny Rome (actually Las Matas outside Madrid) and concerns the choices made by Commodus that triggered the slow decline of the empire.

Director Mann agreed the film was dark, and partly attributed its financial failure to the film being "defeatist," so it was difficult for an audience to leave feeling upbeat.

The Story

Marcus Aurelius (Alec Guinness) is near death at Rome's Northern frontier near what is now Austria. He does not trust his son Commodus (Christopher Plummer) to take over as the new Caesar, and tells his daughter Lucilla (Sophiia Loren) that Livius (Stephen Boyd), commander of the Army, should succeed him. Aurelius talks of a vast Pax Romana, where all the countries Rome has conquered can live in peace. Borders between countries would vanish, and he begins to talk of '"human" frontiers.

Meanwhile, a plot to kill Aurelius is hatching. Not content to let Aurelius die naturally, some of Aurelius' inner circle wants Commodus to become Emperor immediately. They concoct and execute a scheme to poison Aurelius with an apple.

The Emperor dies, and rather than harm the empire with a power struggle, Livius steps aside for Commodus to become Caesar. In a stunning sequence shot in a snowstorm with Northern Spain substituting for the Austrian frontier, Aurelius is cremated and Commodus assumes the throne.

After a triumphal entry into a sunny Rome (the first shot in the film taken in bright light), Commodus begins immediately to undo all the uniting that his father had accomplished. He raises taxes, unfairly burdening the Roman provinces. Commodus is advised that this stranglehold will only foster rebellion, but Commodus is unmoved. It is in these moments that the seeds of Rome's destruction are seen to begin taking root.

Commodus uses the Roman legions to hammer away at the provinces, but revolt is in the air. While rebellion grows, Commodus spends time in the arena as a gladiator, and preparing new and lavish entertainments for Roman citizens.

Livius appears before the Senate to argue for policies more in line of Aurelius', but the Senate, now virtually under Commodus' control, will hear nothing of it.

Livius prepares the army to march into Rome, but Commodus showers money on the army to disband. It's a successful ploy. Livius is arrested as a traitor along with Lucilla and others who were enemies of Commodus.

Commodus orders his enemies chained to stakes at the center of the Roman Forum, where it is planned they will be burned.

In a supreme moment of ego, Commodus offers to fight Livius

to the death at the center of the Roman Forum. The victor becomes Caesar, and the Gods would decide who wins.

After a well-staged javelin and swordfight, Livius triumphs, but refuses the offer to become Caesar and walks away, rescuing Lucilla and leaving the title of Emperor to the fate of an auction.

The bright skies are covered now with dark smoke from the bodies that have been burned, and the narrator tells us that great empires die not from outside forces, but from within.

The History

The Fall of the Roman Empire, correctly, I think, places the beginnings of the fall of Rome at the transition between Aurelius and Commodus. Rome's last good emperor, Aurelius, hands the throne to Commodus, generally thought of as the one emperor that nothing good can be said about.

The plot does deviate in part from generally accepted history. Although some writers suggest Aurelius was poisoned, there is no evidence for it. It is generally thought he died of plague.

Commodus was the true son of Caesar, not illegitimate as portrayed in the film as the son of Caesar's wife and a gladiator.

And the real Commodus was much worse than the strutting egomaniac portrayed in the film. He did fight in the arena (more than 700 times) and always won because the fights were fixed. He was nineteen when he took the throne, often appearing with blood on his skin or clothing for effect and he charged the Roman treasury for each gladiator spectacle. He had a harem of 300 young men and women to satisfy his pleasures.

The role of Livius in the film is an invented character, and Commodus' sister Lucilla was real, but not the moral person described in the film. In fact, she was among those plotting Commodus' death, which came, not at a duel in the Roman forum, but by his being poisoned, then strangled in his bathtub.

The alternate history devised by the writers works very well dramatically, and, in fact, was largely lifted by Ridley Scott for *Gladiator*, which has Commodus kill Aurelius, and ends with a fight in the arena between Commodus and Maximus, another made up character. Norma Barzman, whose husband was the chief writer of the film, found it interesting that the Scott film, perhaps using *Fall* for a model, got the history wrong in exactly the same way.

The Production

Writing in 1964, director Anthony Mann said, "The film was origi-nally my idea. I was walking down Picadilly and I passed Hachard's bookshop and saw the Oxford concise edition of the *Decline and Fall* in the window. I had just finished *El Cid* and said to myself, 'now what would make an interesting picture?' Samuel Bronston wanted me to direct another epic for him so I took him the subject and said I had no idea what the story was going to be, but would he let me work on it." [Mann, quoted in *Films and Filming*, 1964]

Bronston was enthusiastic about the idea. *The Fall of the Roman Empire* was to be the film that followed *El Cid*, but when Heston balked and said he instead liked the under development *55 Days at Peking*, Bronston tore down the Roman Forum set that was begin-ning construction and replaced it with the Forbidden City. With that completed, the Forbidden City sets were pulled down and the Roman Forum replaced it.

By any definition, the Forum was an incredible set. Built with the guidance of historian Will Durant, the Colasanti and Moore Forum is still one of the largest sets ever built for a motion picture. At 1312 by 754 feet it was not extended with matte paintings the way other sets like *Ben-Hur* were. What you see on the screen was all physically built, not just false fronts, but dimensional build-ings. (*Troy*, made in 2003, claimed a larger outdoor set, but much of it was computer enhanced.) The set was built on the plains of Las Matas, about 16 miles from the Bronston Studios in Madrid. Bronston wanted not just a set, but a full scale duplicate of the Roman Forum that Commodus himself would recognize. Accord-ing to studio publicity, more than 3,000 sketches were made of the 27 structures that would comprise the set.

Construction began on October 1, 1962 using 1,100 men who labored for seven months. About 400 art students and craftsmen from all over Spain worked on the statuary, tiles, frescoes and de-tail of the sets.

To get the Temple of Jupiter the right height, workmen con-structed a 95-foot-high hill on the plains of Las Matas, and then built the 165-foot-high temple on it. The bronze equestrian figures at the top of the temple were 260 feet above the pavement of the forum set.

Bronston's craftsmen also had a huge assignment just for statu-ary. Three hundred and fifty statues had to be constructed. There were 76 life-size statues, more than a thousand sculptured bases for the remaining figures and victory columns, and a series of the afore-mentioned equestrian statues that were 25 feet high. Interior scenes were shot in Madrid at Bronston studios, and at Cinecitta in Rome where Commodus' baths and gymnasiums were constructed.

Studio publicity touted some amazing numbers: 170,000 large pavement blocks for the Roman Forum set, 610 columns for the buildings, 22,000 feet of concrete for steps, ramps and stairways, 24,000 pounds of nails, 33,000 gallons of paint and 230,000 roofing tiles.

After the set was mostly pulled down, some remaining frag-ments were used in Richard Lester's *A Funny Thing Happened on the*

Way to the Forum. The Bronston Studios get a mention in the film credits. While Bronston might have been able to rent the set out for other productions, he felt he had created something unique for his film, and did not want to see the vistas he had created exploited by other filmmakers.

Samuel Bronston's son Bill told me it was astounding to stand on those sets, and feel real stone under your feet, not plaster. No expense was spared, and it showed. Only one quick image detracts from the illusion, a shot taken from the high ground near the Temple of Jupiter that shows the Roman citizens running toward Commodus. One can see between the edifices, a bare horizon, the flat Spanish plains of Las Matas, rather than a teeming ancient city.

The costuming and interior sets are also first rate. With Colasanti and Moore combing archives, paintings and frescoes for ideas, the look of reality drips off the screen. There was probably no other Roman epic to look so rich, or so real.

Bronston was proud of the craftsmanship on all his films. He bragged to distributors that nothing was rented; everything was constructed and created by local talent. It was done the same way as *El Cid* before it, and it allowed the film to look striking, far beyond what had been done in other films with producers and craftsmen less committed to accuracy.

Yakima Canutt did the stunts for the film as he had done for *El Cid*, and excelled on the chariot race and in the battles with the barbarian hordes. His work began five months before the actual filming began. One of his first tasks was to round up 1,500 horses from Spain and Portugal and train them on how to work before the camera, as well as learn to fall safely during the battle scenes.

A major undertaking for Canutt and director Mann was to set up the battle between the Romans and Persians so the 8,000 extras being used would show up on screen.

During production, Mann was quoted as saying, "If you stretch out thousands of soldiers on a flat terrain, those in the rear are so diminished by distance that you lose the effect of their numbers. To avoid this, we located a corrugated plain near Manzanares El Real. When the soldiers battled over the undulating plain, those in the rear were elevated into better view of the cameras and their numbers seemed endless in the scene."

The chariot race for the film was thrilling and a difficult shoot. Canutt's son Tap doubled for Stephen Boyd, while Jack Williams substituted for Christopher Plummer. The race takes place on a winding road cut out of a mountain. One side of the road drops off to a small river flowing about a hundred feet below.

In the film, Plummer tries to run Boyd's chariot off the road, so Canutt reinforced the chariots and allowed one of the wheels to slip off the road, hanging in space. Eventually, the fight leaves the road for a dense pine forest, and the chariots flip after hitting a ramp Canutt's team placed in the chariot's path. It was a far different chariot race than the one Canutt shot in *Ben-Hur*; it was shorter and not confined to an arena. It is an exciting scene, and remarkably no one was seriously injured during the filming.

The script was by Basilio Franchina and Ben Barzman, both of whom had worked together on *El Cid*. For *Fall*, they would work in a similar way, with Franchina doing a lot of the research, Barzman doing the bulk of the actual screenplay. If some of Marcus Aurelius' lines seem lyrical and authentic, they should. Some of his dialog is taken from his actual writings.

Other scenes stay with the viewer long after the film is over. The debate in the Roman Senate is the moral center of the film, as Livius tries to preserve Aurelius' dream of Pax Romana, but many of the Roman Senators want to use Roman force to dictate the future of the empire. It leads one of the Senators, Caecina, played by *Ben-Hur* veteran Finlay Currie, to ask, "We have changed the world - can we not change ourselves?"

Mann said he did not want just spectacle, and he worked hard to bring characters to the drama. "I have concentrated in the first part on establishing the characters in simple, human terms - meeting characters doing the things they did in those days, the sacrifice of a bird, or simple things we would do in our everyday lives. Then the spectacle is done entirely differently to what you would expect, because the whole of the empire comes to Marcus Aurelius in the mountains with all their different colored chariots, their different religions, and so on; and he makes a speech to them, and the speech is what the empire was - so that in very simple terms we show the empire and its vastness though the eyes of one man. The story is told through the eyes of individuals rather than having chunks of character and spectacle in between. The first half of the picture is an intimate story of life and death, and the characters bring you into the spectacle, rather than it being imposed on you without dramatic reason." [Anthony Mann in *Films and Filming*, 1964]

In fact, the film is constructed in two distinct parts - the darker *noir-ish* beginning, which last for a bit more than an hour, and then the brighter drama in Rome, where Commodus rules with ruthless determination. It is in Rome that the difference between father and son is brought to light, and the seeds of Rome's destruction are sown.

Fall has a far different tone from so many of the epics that came before it. There is no Christianity in this Roman epic. The empire is beginning to rot from within, and early Christianity is not the catalyst; this in keeping with Durant, who saw the rise of Christianity as more of "an effect than cause of Rome's decay." [Durant, *Caesar and Christ*, page 665-67.] Clearly, this was not to be an epic like *Ben-Hur* or *Quo Vadis?*, with the Romans against the Christians. This is Rome set upon Rome, battling for survival against its own dissipation and invaders from without.

Anthony Mann made it clear: "I did not want to make another *Quo Vadis*, or *Spartacus* [which Mann directed until he fell out with producer Kirk Douglas and was replaced by Stanley Kubrick], or any of the others because these stories were the stories of the Christ. Those films gave the impression that the Christian movement was the only thing the Roman Empire was about, but it was a minor incident in the greatness of the Roman Empire." [*Films and Filming*, 1964]

Mann was also a great believer in shooting on location where it was feasible, because the actors could get more emotion and realism into their roles. "I had always thought for Roman Empire, I would love to do the death of Marcus Aurelius in the snow. One morning I woke up and it was *really* snowing. So I called everybody early and I got them up there and I said: 'I know it's freezing to death here, but we'll put you in warm tents and we're going to do this sequence all in the snow.' It was marvelous! Because it had a silence about it, a kind of majesty it wouldn't have had if it had been done on a sunny day or any other kind of day." [Quoted from a Mann interview in *Screen Magazine*, 1964]

The Cast

Casting *The Fall of the Roman Empire* was not a smooth process. Originally designed as a vehicle to reunite Charlton Heston and Sophia Loren, Heston did not feel the script he was presented was up to his standards. He also wasn't anxious to play in another Roman costumer so close to *Ben-Hur*.

Stephen Boyd wound up with the job. Boyd was born in 1931 in Northern Ireland, and had a succession of TV parts in the UK, Canada and the United States before getting his first major screen role in *The Man Who Never Was* (1956). He, of course, played a major lead in *Ben-Hur*, but was not always careful about the roles he accepted. One career low point was when he played Jamuga in the 1965 *Ghengis Khan,* reuniting with Omar Sharif and James Mason who worked with him on *Fall*. As time progressed, Boyd never had a role as good as Messala in *Ben-Hur,* and finished his career roles in TV shows like *Hawaii Five-0* and minor films like *Lady Dracula*. Boyd died in 1977 of a massive heart attack in California.

Sophia Loren was born in Italy in 1934. She was discovered by producer Carlo Ponti at a beauty contest, and went on to act in dozens of Italian films before she was known to a worldwide audience. In 1960 she won a Best Actress Oscar in De Sica's *Two Women*. Notably, she was paid a million dollars to star in *Fall*, the second woman to collect that fee for a film, after Elizabeth Taylor got the same paycheck for *Cleopatra* (1963).

Richard Harris was originally cast as Commodus, but withdrew. As it turned out, the young Christopher Plummer steals every scene he is in. Commodus was an early film role for Plummer, who had previously worked mainly in television. Bronston saw Plummer in a London stage production of *Becket*, and knew that Plummer would be good in the role. Plummer is terrific as Commodus, and we see him slowly going mad as the film progresses. This is Plummer before his role in *The Sound of Music* made him famous (or infamous). He went on to a strong career (*The Insider, Syriana, A Beautiful Mind*) that has spanned more than 40 years. He is probably the one actor along with Alec Guinness that leaves an indelible impression when the film is over.

The film works well when Alec Guinness and James Mason are on screen. Guinness does a good turn as Aurelius, but he is killed off early. The part did not have much impact on the actor. In his autobiography he hardly mentions it, and when he does he says he only saw 20 minutes of the finished film.

Guinness was born in London in 1914. He earned an Oscar for his work in *The Bridge on the River Kwai* in 1957, and had memorable roles in *The Lavender Hill Mob* (1951), *The Ladykillers* (1955), *Our Man in Havana* (1959) and *Lawrence of Arabia* (1962). He died in 2000.

James Mason was born in Yorkshire England in 1909. Two roles, *The Seventh Veil* (1945) and *Odd Man Out* (1947), made Mason an international star, and he moved to Hollywood in 1949. Other notable roles for Mason were as Captain Nemo in *20,000 Leagues Under the Sea* (1954) and *Lolita* (1962). Mason acted in several epic films, including *Julius Caesar* (1953), *Prince Valiant* (1954) *Lord Jim* (1965), and *Genghis Khan* (1965). Mason died in 1984.

Other actors of note were Anthony Quayle (*Guns of Navarone* and *Lawrence of Arabia*) and John Ireland (*Raw Deal*, directed by Anthony Mann, *Red River*, *All the Kings Men* and Bronston's *55 Days at Peking*). Omar Sharif (*Lawrence of Arabia, Mackenna's Gold, The Last Valley, Doctor Zhivago*) has a small part in the film with only a few minutes of screen time. Sharif plays the husband in a marriage arranged for Lucilla by Marcus Aurelius. In his autobiography, his role in the film gets only a brief mention. He does remember his six months in Spain, mainly playing poker with Sophia Loren to pass the time.

The Music

Dimitri Tiomkin wrote the score for the film. Tiomkin, who had won three Oscars for the scores to *High Noon, High and the Mighty* and *The Old Man and the Sea*, was a bombastic and highly energetic composer. He did not write "traditional" epic music, and made no attempt, as Rozsa had done in *King of Kings* and *El Cid*, to compose a score that sounded archaic or ancient. Instead, he wrote passionate music with a full palette of orchestral colors augmenting the standard instruments with a large brass choir and an organ.

In liner notes for the soundtrack Tiomkin wrote: "I decided I must dismiss all ideas of giving this picture quasi-documentary style music. My plan was to react spontaneously to the dramatic element which I gradually began to appreciate in *Roman Empire*. I excitedly started to block important dramatic and lyrical passages and found myself, to my great surprise, involved not with characters from eighteen centuries ago, but with characters whose problems were remarkably like our own and practically coincidental with all human drama. They were amazingly alive, close to me ... and then the melodies started to come."

Tiomkin's craft is evident throughout the film. When the film was originally screened it had a powerful musical overture, with antiphonal brass choirs coming from the left and right side of the screen. The opening titles feature an orchestra with organ previewing the dark spectacle of the film. He brings to life the Pax Romana segment where armies from throughout the Roman Empire pay tribute to Aurelius. Tiomkin writes an uplifting, repeating melody as each army leader rides to the foreground to pledge loyalty. For the end of the film, Tiomkin revives the organ music and orchestra as dark billows of smoke portray the empire's fall. Tiomkin's score for *The Fall of the Roman Empire* received an Oscar nomination for best music score, and won the Golden Globe for best original score.

Final Thoughts

> "If you listen very closely, you can hear the gods laughing"
> - Christopher Plummer as Commodus

The Fall of the Roman Empire is a magnificent production. From the early shots of the Empire's frigid northern borders to the end at the Roman Forum set, the film is spectacular. The care in costuming, set design, and props are obvious. No film before or since looked as opulent, nor was such an effort made to get things right.

While the script is intelligent, the dark atmosphere likely did not appeal to filmgoers. The overall feel of the film is dark. It was not what moviegoers expected to see, and there were not many moviegoers who went to see it. It may have been fatigue from all the prior epics. *Cleopatra* had just been out the year before, and the pre-launch publicity for that film may have hurt the genre as a whole.

Publicity for the Bronston film emphasized the big crowd scenes and the chariot race; images that may have made the film look like a retread *of Ben-Hur*. Having Stephen Boyd in the cast couldn't have helped. When the action scenes with battles and a chariot race were previewed, the film may have looked too derivative of *Ben-Hur*. This was probably heightened by the corny and inappropriate publicity campaign.

The film also sported one of the worst, inappropriate trailers ever conceived for a film, saying the story contained "all the known emotions." I don't think anyone seeing that trailer would have been interested in going to see the film it promoted in such a heavy-handed way.

It wasn't because Mann did not try. In fact, he made the film to be more about people, and played down the epic parts of the story. He thought the relationship between Commodus and Marcus Aurelius was the heart of the picture, telling *Screen Magazine*, "He [Commodus] tries to kill his father's image, because this image is greater than his own. This is the story underneath the Oedipus drama. I don't know of any great man who ever had a great son. This must have been a terrible thing for the son - to live with the image of his father, for although this is a love-image, it can also be a hate-image. This theme is recurrent, because it is a very strong one and, consequently, I like it - it reaches to heights and depths beyond more mundane stories."

The film is also very long. At more than three hours it is a long haul for an unhappy ending. As long as the movie is, it could have been even longer. Bill Bronston says about 40 minutes were cut out, including a lengthy scene of Commodus and Livius drinking and talking about the old days, and there is also evidence of scenes that show Lucilla directly involved in an attempt on Commodus' life. That would be historically accurate, but the scene, for which Tiomkin composed music, was cut. Those missing 40 minutes are probably lost, but Bill Bronston believes some of the very heart of the film was left on the cutting room floor.

Will Durant expressed displeasure with the finished film. Although he was thrilled with the look and accuracy of the sets, he felt the story departed too much from history.

As has been pointed out, the key writers and director had also done *El Cid*, yet in *Fall*, for all the things done well, the magic from *El Cid* was missing. I asked Norma Barzman, whose late husband wrote both films, want went wrong. "They didn't have any thing substantial to work with. You know, the fall of Rome, what did it take, hundreds of years? I don't think it was a good story. It wasn't a good story and it didn't play out well and you didn't care about anybody.

"The romance in the film doesn't work. You don't care about anybody. That's one of the few things that Ben's written that, even things that were lesser you cared more about the people, it was more dramatic, it had more of a story, it was better. That is just a mess as far as I'm concerned."

Barzman and some others may be too condemning. She hasn't seen the film for more than 40 years, and some notable critics have been very kind to it. My own view is that it does not have the magic of *El Cid*, but it has drama, conflict, spectacle and intelligence. It is marred by a weak performance by Boyd, which undercuts any power his romance with Sophia Loren might have had. We never get to know either of them, or their backstory, so there is little for the audience to feel. Boyd is almost robotic, and Loren seems to mainly cry. The romance drags down any chance of emotional connection for those characters. If Heston had taken the role, he would have pushed the writers for better material.

One wonders if George Lucas saw Guinness in *Fall* and modeled the character of Obi-Wan Kenobi after him for *Star Wars* in 1977? They look and dress the same. In fact, coincidence or not, some of the overall mythology of *Star Wars* has seeds that took root in *Fall*. It is the thesis of an extended article by Martin Winkler in *Classical Myth and Culture in the Cinema* (Oxford University Press 2001). In his essay, Winkler finds parallels to *Fall* in the character Guinness plays in both films, and even links the Speeder race through the forest in *The Empire Strikes Back* to the chariot race through the forest in *Fall*. His thesis seems to be a bit of a stretch on first reading, but one can see the connections, and they may be more than happenstance as so many of Lucas' films are drawn from prior scripts and literature.

At the time of its release, critics had seen enough epics and were generally negative. Bosley Crowther in the *New York Times* said, "So massive and incoherent is it, so loaded with Technicolored spectacles, tableaus and military melees that have no real meaning or emotional pull, that you're likely to have the feeling after sitting through its more than three hours (not counting time out for intermission), that the Roman Empire has fallen on you."

Mann always liked the film, and felt he needed to defend it against some of the more raspy critics. "Now I guarantee you there is not one person that had read Gibbon . . . From Bosley Crowther on down or up. And for them to start to say: 'This isn't Gibbon'

- well, this is a lot of crap! Because all we were trying to do was dramatize how an empire fell. Incest, buying an army, destroying the will of the people to speak through the Senate, all these things . . . were in the film."

Variety was kinder. "The production reeks of expense - harness and hay for all those horses, arroz con pollo for all those Spanish extras, annuities for all those stars. Attention will focus upon the marblesque replica of downtown Rome in pagan days with temples, squares, forums, statuary, mosaic floors, columned chambers, luxury suites and a plunge for Caesar. If these sets cost a fortune, they pay off in stunning camera angles."

In England, the *Daily Express* called it "an epic to make one cheer rather than cringe" and the *Evening Standard* critic proclaimed it "one of the best all-round epics I have ever seen."

As years went on, the reviews have gotten warmer. George Chabot, writing in 2000, said, "The movie continually gets better as it goes, nearly three hours in running time. While Stephen Boyd was probably not the best choice for the lead, he did a creditable job at depicting rectitude in the midst of excess and I enjoyed his performance very much. Omar Sharif played the King of Armenia, Sophia Loren's husband. Anthony Quayle played the gladiator trainer. James Mason played a Roman Senator. Christopher Plummer played the evil emperor Commodus. John Ireland played a barbarian chieftain. The cast was absolutely brilliant with great performances all around."

Jon Solomon, writing in *The Ancient World in the Cinema* (Yale University Press, 2001), says that "the impressive double decked square of thick shields in which Commodus and Livius fight to the death, the gigantic hand of Sabazius in the forum from which the divine Commodus emerges, the exciting chariot race in the snow, and Commodus' lavish baths - all merit more appreciation than they received in the wake of the *Cleopatra* debacle."

Overall, for me, the film works. I like the dark and foreboding opening sections. The funeral of Aurelius in the snow is pure and chilling cinema. The cut to the Roman Forum scenes, as Commodus enters Rome, is also notable. Starting on a tight shot of the Forum, cinematographer Robert Krasker slowly pans and opens up the shots so we get the full impact of the massive forum set. We also see the tremendous cast of extras. It is a thrilling tableau, and while current movies like *Gladiator* and *Kingdom of Heaven* have big scenes, largely done with computer graphics, the impact is not the same.

As good as the forum set is, it may have been over used. According to Norma Barzman, her late husband was forced to re-write scenes and move them to the Forum so the expensive set would get more exposure. "[Executive Producer] Mike Waszynski really only intervened to say, 'You've got to use that set we spent a million dollars on. You've got to use it more to show it was worthwhile.' That's the only kind of intercession that he made. He didn't intercede to say how the story should go. He only said it was really to prove that he had done the right thing by ordering those extra sets."

What we're left with is a film that reached for dramatic and cinematic heights, but did not always reach the mark. It was lovingly put together, and told a difficult and unhappy story about the end of an empire. It was not a story the public ultimately wanted to see, but today the film gets better and better notices. It is available in Europe and Asia on DVD, and I'm happy to say it is scheduled be released in the United States on DVD by the Weinstein Company in the early part of 2008. As I have mentioned earlier Bill Bronston and I have done the commentary to further illuminate the stories behind the making of this epic film. I hope the movie finds a new generation of fans that will connect to its message and be amazed at this intelligent and spectacular motion picture.

Bill Bronston told me it is much like other films his dad made with a loving attention to detail and an attempt to make something really special. "That was the same thing in all of his movies. They used as much original material as they possibly could. There was always a very serious preoccupation with striving for authenticity. They really did reach for authenticity and reliability, and they spared no expense to find people who were really authorities."

Martin Scorsese, writing about *Fall*, said "it has the poignant beauty of a lost art."

It would be impossible to make a film like *Fall* today, and, of course, in retrospect it appears to have been a mistake to have made it in 1964, coming as it did at the end of the cycle of epic films. Viewing it now, separated by decades from the time of its release, *The Fall of the Roman Empire* looks more like the classic it was intended to be. While not a perfect film, *The Fall of the Roman Empire* today is enjoyable to watch. No one had focused on this part of Roman History before for a film, no one had made the effort to get the look of sets, locations and costumes as precisely as Bronston and his team. It is dark, and depressing, but so then was the real Fall of Rome.

Fall was not an optimistic film like *El Cid*. One feels angry and bitter at the end, watching the promise of Rome drift away in the burning smoke. To filmgoers who just lived through the Kennedy assassination and the escalating war in Southeast Asia, the message was probably too somber and certainly not escapism. Top grossing films released the same year were *Mary Poppins* and *My Fair Lady*, while *The Fall of the Roman Empire*, which cost Bronston and Paramount almost 20 million dollars to produce, was the studio's biggest flop of 1964.

Seeing the film recently is, I think, a fresh experience. Of all the Bronston films, however, it is probably the most polarizing. Some critics and people who remember it call it a masterpiece, with epic proportions and an intellectual script trying to tackle the fall of Rome in a couple of hours of screen time. Others see it as over-blown, lacking depth and any characters that filmgoers could care about. Even Ben Barzman, principal writer of the film, did not like how it turned out.

Alec Guinness said he could barely remember it, and briefly re-ferred to it in his book, *Blessings in Disguise*: "While flying out to Spain, I sat gazing forlornly at the script and jotting down a few notes. A tall American came to sit beside me and asked if I was studying my lines. 'Well, re-writing them, where possible,' I said. 'What do you think of the script?' he asked. 'Not much,' I replied . . . It was tact-less of me; I didn't realize until I met him later that my companion was the scriptwriter. The saving grace - apart from Anthony Mann, who was a friendly director and well-disposed towards actors - was Sophia Loren, whose company I enjoyed enormously."

All the critics did agree, however, that the production values were of the highest quality, and that ancient Rome truly comes alive in the film.

There has been resurgence of late with many historians talking about the fall of Rome in context of western civilizations' current challenges. In the United States, people wonder if our country is over extended and has become arrogant and bogged down in for-eign wars and adventures. Such considerations could make the ideas on *The Fall of the Roman Empire* resonate with a new genera-tion. When the film is re-released on DVD in America, with wide-screen, multi-channel sound and a restored print, a new genera-tion may find a deep significance within the film that was missing in 1964. They could also get a look at the progenitor of *Gladiator* and, in my view, see a better film from Bronston.

As the historical Rome fell, The *Fall of the Roman Empire* represented the fall of the epic film. Too expensive, too repetitive of what came before it. This film marked a sad turning point for the Bronston organization. Flush with the success of *El Cid*, Bronston thought that this film could not miss. *55 Days at Peking*, which was rushed into production when Heston chose that over appearing in *Fall*, did very well in Europe, and took in fair box office in the United States. Bronston was hopeful that teaming so many of the people that made *El Cid* a hit was bound to guarantee another smash.

Paramount took the U.S. distribution rights for the first time in a Bronston film, and proudly told the trade press that they were excited to have the Bronston epic because they were the studio that had produced the DeMille blockbusters. Their happiness did not last long as receipts came in, and they knew they were already committed to Bronston's next film, *Circus World* with John Wayne.

The experience of *The Fall of the Roman Empire* killed any future spectacles about Rome, and certainly made it far more difficult for producers to turn out large epics on any historical subject. *Mutiny on the Bounty*, made at about the same time, almost destroyed MGM, and *Cleopatra* almost wiped out 20th Century-Fox. The studios knew they needed big films to compete with television, which was now broadcasting almost completely in color. But they struggled with getting the right properties and methods to keep costs under control.

Seen today, *The Fall of the Roman Empire* looks awfully good. It is a product of another time, and another method of creating big screen entertainment. While far from a perfect film, it excites the senses and takes us to another time and another place. We get to see as close a replica of ancient Rome as we are ever likely to see, and we see a movie produced in a way that would simply be impossible today. While the script does not match the quality of the production design, the writers had an almost impossible task to turn 300 years of history into a coherent, compact three hours of screen time.

Bronston's epic combines triumph and tragedy: The triumph of recreating the splendor of ancient Rome, the tragedy of bad timing by bringing out a film when the public didn't care if it ever saw another toga, a Roman army on the march, or another chariot race.

Circus World

"A Big screen, big box office spectacle."

Screenplay: Ben Hecht, Julian Halevy [Julian Zimet] and James Edward Grant, **Story**: Philip Yordan and Nicholas Ray; **Director**: Henry Hathaway; Producer: Samuel Bronston; **Cast**: John Wayne, Claudia Cardinale, Rita Hayworth, Lloyd Nolan, Richard Conte, John Smith, Hans Dantes, Wanda Rotha, Miles Malleson, Katherine Kath. **Released by**: Paramount Pictures; **Running time**: 135 minutes. Shot in Super Technirama 70 (Aspect Ratio 2.20: 1)

Circus World was a complete departure from the tone of the previous Bronston epics. The idea had been kicked around for a long time, with various writers working on ideas.

Bernard Gordon, who wrote much of the script for *55 Days at Peking*, came up with the idea. In a 2006 interview, Gordon told me, "Well, that was another project where [Phil] Yordan said, 'You know, we have to have another big picture.' And I said, 'Let's do a circus picture but just hold it, not the kind we usually do with the lion tamer and the girl and so on, all that crap.' I said, 'Let's do something where, we're here in Europe, let's go all around Europe, to all the different places, and do spectacular acts, a man is going to pull together for a circus, spectacular acts, which would be very promotable.' And in order to get that done, my idea was to get this American circus going to Europe on a ship and the ship starts to sink and they lose most of their animals and most of their acts, and he comes to Europe and he's got to put together a whole new circus from scratch, which would put him all around the world, to the acts of people working on tightropes, you know, from one building to another, and so on. And that's how we started on *Circus World*. I did a draft of that."

The draft is essentially what the picture became. It went through three directors, starting with Nicholas Ray, who was mulling over the film after *55 Days at Peking*. From there it went on to Frank Capra (*It's a Wonderful Life, Mr. Smith Goes to Washington*), but Capra did not get along with the Bronston people, and they did not get along with Capra, who was working far too slowly for their taste. Finally, it wound up with Henry Hathaway (*Desert Fox, North to Alaska, How the West Was Won, True Grit*), and did nothing to enhance the careers of anyone who got near it. It was an inexpensive film by Bronston standards, budgeted at about nine million dollars. But after the 28 million spent on *The Fall of the Roman Empire*, no one was anxious to bankroll another big Bronston film.

In many ways, the film seemed out of character for Bronston, whose previous movies had been stories of legendary heroes and bigger-than-life historical events. *Circus World* essentially was about a down-and-out Circus owner trying to put his circus and his life back together. True, the star was the larger-than-life John Wayne, but a larger-than-life actor does not make a story an epic. To pump up the epic qualities the film opened with the spectacular sinking of the circus ship, but it probably came too early in the film and set up expectations for more thrills. Other than the fire scenes as the Big Top goes up in smoke at the end of the picture, there weren't any other scenes that excited audiences. Frankly, the picture committed the cardinal sin: It was boring and the characters were flat.

One other notable item about the film is that it was marketed as a Cinerama film and opened in Cinerama theaters. Shot in the Super Technirama process, it was a far cry from the original three-strip Cinerama process that debuted in the 1950s.

Circus World was shot originally in 35mm Technirama, and then blown up to 70mm for projection on a curved screen using an anamorphic lens. The process did fill a large screen, but was far less involving than true Cinerama could ever be and it was a fraction of the resolution. Philip Yordan, long an associate of Bronston, struck out on his own and also used the same process for *Custer of the West.*

The Story

John Wayne plays impresario Matt Masters, who wants to take his Circus and Wild West show to Europe. He has another motive, and that is to find Lili Alfredo (Rita Hayworth), his long lost love who disappeared years before when her husband died during a high-wire act. She left Masters to raise her child, Toni, played by Claudia Cardinale. It's hinted that her husband's death might have been a suicide when he learned Lili was in love with Masters. In the early parts of the film, none of this backstory is known to Toni, who views Matt as a loving stepfather who has taken care of her since she was a little girl.

Cap Carson (Lloyd Nolan), a close friend of Masters, tries to talk him out of the European tour, and knows about Masters' feelings for Lili, but Matt insists the tour is a good idea financially.

Matt and his crew load the animals and performers on a ship, the *Circus Maximus*, at the Brooklyn Naval Yard for the trip across the Atlantic for their first stop at Barcelona.

When they arrive, one of the circus performers does a high-wire act on a wire set up in the rigging of the ship as the public watches from the dock and the deck of the ship. An accident occurs, and the performer winds up in the water.

As spectators quickly move to one side of the ship, the weight is too much and the ship begins listing and then winds up on its side throwing hundreds of spectators and caged animals into Barcelona Harbor.

Panic follows, but all are rescued by Matt and his circus staff and performers, and there are no fatalities, but most of the circus animals are lost and Masters has little left of his dream.

Desperate for cash, Matt, Cap, and his other close associates head for Paris and join another circus, Colonel Purdy's Wild West Show. Matt does some spectacular stunts on a runaway stagecoach with Toni's boyfriend, Steve McCabe (John Smith). The stunts are a hit, and Masters and his crew are written up in the Paris newspapers as a sensation.

The success compels Masters to try and relaunch his own circus, taking his stagecoach act as a start and signing more acts as he travels through Europe.

He then plans to winter in Spain getting his own circus ready to complete the European tour that ended with the sinking of his ship.

The tour begins, with Matt taking the troupe to Brussels, Milan, and finally Madrid. At one performance, Lili is there, watching the daughter she has not seen in years. She approaches Matt, and they reunite, with Lili wanting to join the circus as a trapeze artist but wants an assurance from Matt that he will not reveal to Toni that she is Toni's mother.

Of course, one of the circus clowns (Richard Conte) reveals to Toni that Lili is her mother, and Toni becomes angry at Masters for the years of deceit.

A fire breaks out in the big circus tent, and is put out before too much damage is done. Many of the main characters risk their lives to save the circus, and Toni's anger subsides as she hugs her mother and Masters and they feel they are a family for the first time.

Tony marries Steve McCabe, and now there is a new circus, the Masters and McCabe Combined International Circus.

The Production

To make a circus movie, Bronston needed a circus, so he hired Franz Althoff, one of an illustrious family of Circus managers and performers. Althoff Circuses are still popular around the world today, most notably in Europe.

Bronston not only got Althoff, he also got 400 members of his cast and crew to be part of the movie so it would look authentic. To add further insurance that the circus plot would appear real, Bronston hired Bob Dover, performance director the of Ringling Brothers Circus, Umberto Bedini, Ringling's chief booker for circus acts, and Alfredo Marquerie, an expert on circuses as well as a critic and journalist. Bronston studio publicity said that Marquerie had gained notoriety by entering a lion cage with a microphone an interviewing Dola, a famous lion tamer.

The spectacular scene in the film is undoubtedly the capsizing of the vessel *Circus Maximus* in the Barcelona Harbor. Here's how it was done. First, the Bronston organization secured a ship headed for mothballs, the *S.S. Cabo Huertas*, which had a last voyage planned between the Greek Islands and Barcelona. The ship was repainted, and large circus posters were put on the sides of the 250-foot-long ship. Rigging for the high-wire act that was part of the plot was put into place, along with a swaying 50-foot pole that would be used for a stuntman to be thrown into the water to begin the capsizing sequence.

Special effects man Alex Weldon (*King of Kings*, *El Cid*, and *The Fall of the Roman Empire* for Bronston, as well as *The Wind and the Lion*, *Orca*, *Star Trek: The Motion Picture* and *Raise the Titanic*) was tasked with tipping over the ship, renamed the *Circus Maximus*. The first step was to get fuel oil out of the lower hold, which was divided into two sections of six compartments each. The compartments that were opposite the dock were filled with water, while the compartments closest to the dock were left empty. It took about 300 tons of water to pump half the hold full. Weldon calculated that the weight of the water, plus the added weight of 600 extras lined up at the rail was enough to flip the ship beyond its center of gravity.

To keep the ship upright until it was time for the capsizing, Weldon used four 50-ton steam winches with heavy steel cables attached to the side of the ship that faced the dock, with the cables hidden from the camera. On cue, the cables were released and the ship rolled away from the dock toward the harbor.

Dumping 600 extras into the harbor brought a new set of problems that had to be solved. The wardrobe department fitted the women with corsets made of cork to keep them afloat. For the men in the scene, a wide cork belt that was hidden under their costumes accomplished the same goal.

Bronston got the Spanish Coast Guard involved, and the water was cleared of logs and other debris so actors would not strike any objects in the water. Meanwhile, a fleet of local fisherman and their boats were hired to be just out of camera range to help in the rescue of the waterlogged actors and actresses.

For further insurance, Bronston hired seven divers in scuba gear to patrol the shallow bottom of the harbor in case anyone's cork floats failed.

Amazingly, no one died during this sequence, surprising director Henry Hathaway as much as anyone. "I've been making pictures for 40 years, and this was the greatest job of its kind I have ever been involved in. The fact that we got exactly what we wanted on the screen without a single injury, despite the hazards involved, speaks for itself."

The other big scene in the film is the massive fire in the main Big Top tent. Star John Wayne somehow missed a cue to leave and almost had the burning set fall on top of him. The action in the scene is well staged and well filmed.

The fire and the ship capsizing in the harbor are really the only highlights of the film. The rest is endless exposition and a meandering plot. That being said, Bronston was a man for details, and there was great care taken in the small details of the film.

After hunting all through Europe for a calliope, the film's craftsmen decided to construct one from scratch.

Instead of training horses for the film, Bronston was able to use 125 horses he had already trained for *The Fall of the Roman Empire*. They were used to pull circus wagons, and to carry bareback riders in the grand parade scenes. They received additional training from Joseph Leshkov, who was then one of Europe's premier trainers and riders.

Because the band was supposed to be playing instruments that were current in 1910, the Bronston prop men secured antique instruments from El Escorial, an Iberian city that had preserved the instruments as part of the history of their own city band.

Like some other Bronston productions, this one was troubled. After *55 Days at Peking* Nick Ray was *persona non grata* around the Bronston Studios, and some decided Frank Capra was just the person to direct *Circus World*. Paramount, which was distributing the picture, liked the idea.

Capra had his own ideas. "Bronston was looked up to as one

of the most incredible characters in an incredible business - an elegant gracious old world combination of the financial wizardry of Ponzi, the flamboyant salesmanship of Barnum, and the largesse of Diamond Jim Brady. But all these qualities were secondary to a plaintive childlike compulsion - he wanted everyone to love him." [Capra in the *Name Above the Title*]

Love was not an emotion Capra would feel during his stay in Madrid. He was told John Wayne would bring an entourage with him on his films, and one important person was Wayne's chosen writer and confidante, James Edward Grant.

Capra was dubious, but told Grant to get to work. According to Capra, Grant responded, "No use writing anything till Wayne gets here. Duke makes his own pictures now. So relax fella. When the Duke gets here, he and I will knock you out a screenplay in a week. All you gotta have in a John Wayne picture is a hoity-toity dame with big tits that Duke can throw over his knees and spank, and a collection of jerks he can smash in the face every five minutes. In between, you fill in with gags, flags and chases. That's all you need, his fans eat it up."

It wasn't a direction Capra wanted to go, so he continued to work on the existing script himself. When Wayne arrived in Spain, he rejected Capra's script as uninteresting and unworkable. It was a choice for Bronston - Capra or Wayne. Exit Capra.

Writer Bernard Gordon told me it was Yordan who had to fire Capra. "Well, to begin with, when Capra, when they knew they couldn't go with Capra and Bronston said to [Philip] Yordan, 'Fire him.' Yordan said, 'I'm not gonna fire Capra. You fire him.' Well, they had a little disagreement about that but finally Yordan .... Bronston didn't know how to handle things like that ... so Yordan went to Capra and said, 'Look, I feel terrible about this but you may have written a great script but nobody understands it here and nobody wants to go ahead with that, so we have to go with somebody else and we have to ask you to leave.' Capra had gotten his first payment of $50,000 already; I think it was a $300,000 deal to direct the picture. So Yordan said, 'We'll pay you off.' And Capra was very nice about it. He said, 'No, I'm not gonna do it. You don't have to pay me off. I'll settle for the $50,000 that I got for the time I put in here.' And he said, 'There's only one thing you could do for me. My wife has been around here and she likes some of the old antique furniture that she sees. So if she buys this furniture would you have it crated and shipped to Los Angeles for me?'

"And Yordan was very happy to say yes, we would, and they did. So Capra went. And then the question was, how are they going to make the hero, John Wayne, want to work in this movie? Well, they had settled for John Wayne, they had a contract with him, but he was not going to go with just any old director, so Yordan went to Portugal to meet with John Wayne on John Wayne's sailboat that he'd brought over from California. And there was a lot of drinking and a lot of cigar smoking and Yordan said, 'Well, Capra's gone, we have to go with somebody else.' And Wayne was very easy to deal with but he said, 'I'm not going to just go with any old director you pick.' But Yordan was ready because they had made a deal with the guy who directed it."

Enter Henry Hathaway. According to Gordon, "Well, that was good enough for him [Wayne], so they made a separate deal for more money for John Wayne. Instead of getting $500,000 I think he got $750,000, and he agreed to do the picture. But now they were in the hands of Hathaway, who was the most pigheaded man in the world. And, again, they had a director who was writing his own script and wouldn't show his pages to anybody, just like it was with Capra. Except that Hathaway did know something about picture making. So then Hathaway, with his script but with some of the ideas that I had originally, they went down to Barcelona, they built a part of a ship, and they had it at the dock there, and turned it over and it looked like it was at sea – it was very well done, except I haven't seen it."

Amazingly, as of 2006 Gordon had never even seen *Circus World*. I brought him a copy to watch, and he said he would but he was not enthusiastic about the prospect.

According to Gordon, "Hathaway was incorrigible. You couldn't say or do anything with him. A friend of mine [Julian Zimet] was working with him down there trying to write whatever they needed for dialogue or a scene or anything else, and he was like me, he was a snob who wanted to make good pictures, and here he was living high off the hog down in Barcelona. The best hotel with the best meals and the best of everything paid for by the company. But he wasn't very happy about it ... he was one of the people who was called on the set all the time because John Wayne wanted him around. And John Wayne, well, he's one of the notoriously reactionary guys in this town, but he was not a fool about filmmaking. He would sit there and play chess with this writer [James Edward Grant] who was another reactionary son of a bitch. Julian, who knew chess, would look at them and Wayne would say, 'What's the matter? You didn't think I knew how to play chess? You don't think I can read without moving my lips?'

"But Wayne was friendly with Julian and at one point he got Julian to rewrite a scene the way he liked it and when Hathaway saw it he threw it out and said, 'Listen,' he said to Julian, 'you don't write one word in this script unless I tell you to. I don't give a shit about John Wayne or anybody else. I'm making this picture and you understand that or you're out.' That was the way it was with Hathaway. So the picture is Hathaway's, except for the good ideas that I introduced into it."

By this time Hathaway had gotten rid of James Edward Grant, but the movie was released with writing credits by Ben Hecht, Julian Halevy [Zimet] and James Edward Grant, with story by Philip Yordan and Nicholas Ray. Today, with adjustments by the writers guild, Gordon, who had been blacklisted in Hollywood, is listed as the writer fronting for Yordan.

The Cast

Bronston was always proud of the name stars he could assemble for his movies, and *Circus World* is no exception.

As always, there were changes in the film's cast as production got under way. David Niven was originally to play Cap Carson, the role that went to Lloyd Nolan. Niven read an early script, did not find much of a role there, and passed on another chance to play in a Bronston role.

Of course, the overwhelming star of the film was John Wayne, who was in the film because he owed Paramount Pictures another role under his contract and Paramount did not have anything in their pipeline for him. Philip Yordan saw a chance to keep Paramount from spending $500,000 for Wayne and not getting a picture, so he and Bronston were happy to throw $750,000 at Wayne. Paramount was happy to not be losing the money, and the studio agreed to Western Hemisphere distribution of *Circus World*, as they had done similarly with *The Fall of the Roman Empire*.

Generally not too picky about what films he did, Wayne was, at that time of his career, even less discriminating because he had spent so much money on *The Alamo* (1960), which bombed so badly at the box office. The Texas historical epic was made for 12 million dollars and took in less than eight million. Wayne had used a lot of his own money to fund the production, so over the next few years he was eager to work. *The Alamo* was written by James

Edward Grant, the same writer Wayne insisted be involved in *Circus World*. He had written a string of Wayne films, including *Hondo, The Commancheros, McLintock!* and *Donovan's Reef.*

John Wayne, of course, was a superstar. Born in Winterset, Iowa, his real name was Marion Morrison. His father was a pharmacist. When he was a young boy, the family moved west as his father tried ranching in the Mojave Desert. When the ranch failed, the family moved to Glendale, California, and the young Marion helped deliver medicine for his father.

As a boy, Marion had a dog named Duke, and he adopted the dog's name as his own nickname.

After a failed attempt to get into Annapolis, Marion went to USC on a football scholarship and began doing odd jobs around the studios.

His first important role was in *The Big Trail* (1930), directed by Raoul Walsh. In that film, he took on the name John Wayne.

After a string of B Westerns in the '30s, John Ford hired Wayne to play the Ringo Kid in *Stagecoach* (1939), which was both a financial and artistic success, and Wayne was hailed as a "new screen find."

By 1949 Wayne was in the top ten of box office champs and on three different occasions he was the number one box office draw in America. His films are legendary, among them hits like *Red River, Fort Apache, Sands of Iwo Jima, She Wore a Yellow Ribbon, Hondo*, and The *High and the Mighty.*

As mentioned, he produced, directed and starred in *The Alamo*, and went on to star in *North to Alaska, Hatari!*, and just after *Circus World* he starred in *In Harm's Way* for Otto Preminger. He was nominated for Oscars three times, and won for *True Grit* in 1970. Wayne died of stomach and lung cancer in 1979.

Claudia Cardinale was billed second in *Circus World*. Born in

Tunisia in 1938, she had appeared in small Italian films until she was noticed internationally in 1962 with a role of Fellini's *8 ½* and Visconti's *The Leopard*, co-starring with Alain Delon and Burt Lancaster. That was followed by more recognition in *The Pink Panther* with David Niven and Peter Sellers. Since *Circus World*, she has had an impressive career, with notable roles in *Once Upon a Time in the West* and *Fitzcarraldo*. She continues to act, primarily in Italian films and TV mini-series.

Rita Hayworth completes the trip of top-billed talent for *Circus World*. She joined the cast after a three-year absence from movie-making and gave Bronston an internationally-known Spanish star for the film.

Born Margarita Carmen Cansino in 1918, she wanted to be a dancer, and was discovered by the head of Fox Studios in 1934. Renamed Rita Hayworth, she appeared in a number of minor Columbia titles. She began getting better roles in the early '40s, notably a loan out to Warner Brothers for *The Strawberry Blonde* and her appearance in *You'll Never Get Rich*, where she co-starred and danced with Fred Astaire. Her role in the 1946 film *Gilda* gave her status as a superstar. From that time on she alternated between musicals and dramas.

She was nominated for a Golden Globe for her performance in *Circus World*.

Although not detected, it appears she had an early onset of Alzheimer's disease in the '60s, which was not diagnosed until 1980. She died in the care of her daughter in 1987.

Lloyd Nolan, born in 1902, had a long career on stage and in film before getting the role of Cab Carson in *Circus World*. He played Captain Queeg in *The Caine Mutiny Court-Martial* on Broadway and in London for 832 performances. He also played the role on television, earning him an Emmy award in 1956. Nolan appeared in more than a hundred motion pictures, most notably in *Guadalcanal Diary, Bataan, A Tree Grows in Brooklyn, Ice Station Zebra, Airport, Earthquake*, and *Hannah and Her Sister*s. He died in 1985 of lung cancer.

Richard Conte, born in 1910, in New Jersey, plays a heavy in *Circus World*, Tojo the Clown, who reveals to Claudia Cardinale the true nature of her mother and her mother's affair with John Wayne's character of Matt Masters. He had been cast in an early Bronston-produced film, *A Walk in the Sun* in 1945 after he was discharged from the service. He had been a Bronston family friend for many years, and Bill Bronston remembers Conte often around his father's house over the years. Conte had notable roles in *Call Northside 777*, with Jimmy Stewart (directed by Henry Hathaway), *They Came to Cordura, Ocean's 11, Tony Rome, Lady in Cement*, with Frank Sinatra, and played a major character in *The Godfather*.

Actor John Smith, who plays rodeo rider Steve McCabe, was born in 1931 in Los Angeles. He was given his first big screen role in Wayne's hit film, *The High and the Mighty*. Wayne recommended Smith for *Circus World*. Smith had also appeared in *We're No Angels, Wichita, Friendly Persuasion*, and the *Bold and the Brave*. Since *Circus World*, Smith acted steadily, mostly in television. He died in 1995.

The Critics

It's said that everyone loves a circus, but that wasn't true for many of the major critics.

Bosley Crowther in *The New York Times* said, "John Wayne is mostly sullen and snarly as the circus owner who also performs with evident nonchalance and disinterest in the robbing-the-stage-coach olio.

"Claudia Cardinale is buxom and brash as his foster daugh-ter, whose unaccountably thick Italian accent is one of the many bewildering inconsistencies, and Rita Hayworth strains herself being soulful as the mother who is found in rags. John Smith makes an artificial suitor, Lloyd Nolan is the sturdy old pal, and Richard Conte does everything a heavy should do to identify himself except hold up a sign.

"Out of regard for Cecil B. DeMille's great circus picture, *The Greatest Show on Earth*, it should be said that this one bears no comparison to it. This one might be labeled the worst."

The *Los Angles Citizen News* said, "It provides a grand show for the whole family and is directed in the grand Hollywood tradition."

Box Office observed that, "Bronston captures the 'feel' of the circus magnificently by using actual backgrounds of European shows."

Newsweek thought that John Wayne "lately looks more and more like a waxworks dummy of himself."

Time magazine suggested "To sit through the film is something like holding an elephant on your lap for 2 hours and 15 minutes." But *Time* did allow that "gaps in the story are filled by some delightful European circus acts and other diversions."

Summing Up

If *Circus World* wasn't the "Greatest Show on Earth," it was a nice try. It was undermined by not having strong characters or a script that set out to delineate them. Circus movies are a tough sell in the U.S., and at the time the picture came out people were getting prime time television shows that showed international circus acts. Why would an audience pay to see the same thing? CBS even ran a show called *Frontier Circus* in 1961-62 starring John Derek and Richard Jaeckel.

John Wayne was just being John Wayne, Rita Hayworth had

an understated role and John Smith was, well, just another John Smith.

Whatever the reasons, the nine-million-dollar film flopped just as bad news was coming in about the box office receipts for *The Fall of the Roman Empire*. Paramount had clearly had enough, along with Rank who had distributed most of the Bronston product in the United Kingdom.

With Bronston's chief backer, Pierre DuPont no longer on board, Bronston plunged toward bankruptcy.

In hindsight, one wonders what about this film appealed to Bronston. Philip Yordan and Nicholas Ray had pushed for the idea, but the film seemed mostly devoid of the signature themes that usually inhabited an epic Bronston film. A circus with financial problems is not exactly the creation of Spain or the fall of Rome, and certainly not the New Testament. If anything, *Circus World* was mundane, with its really big scene of the ship sinking coming in the first third of the film. The rest was circus acts and a fire. *Circus World* couldn't top the other Bronston films for drama or for spectacle, and by any measure was not a great film, although it showed great effort in production.

Although Bronson's name would appear on some smaller films years later, the empire he had worked so hard to create was coming down around him as surely as the Big Top had burned to the ground.

The Rise & Fall
of Samuel Bronston

You've read about the films. Of course, the story of these films is incomplete without the story behind the man who made these films possible.

By any measure, the epic films of Samuel Bronston were extraordinary. Even more so perhaps for a poor boy from the Russian provinces with nothing in his pocket and nothing but ambition to drive him to become one of the most powerful film makers of the sixties.

He attracted some of the best talent from Hollywood and Europe, and forged an empire that had no equal anywhere in the world.

Bronston's films are legendary; please allow me a double meaning here - as Bronston's epics were about legendary heroes, the films themselves have become the stuff of legend. There are several reasons for this, including the big stars involved, the tremendous sets, the gigantic numbers of extras, and the amazing amount of money spent on small details.

Bronston had the Spanish Army at his disposal, as well as the support of the Franco government that less than a decade before had been at odds with the United States and the United Nations.

For *El Cid* alone Bronston had somehow arranged the loan of 3,000 Spanish Infantry troops and horses. Not only the troops, but members of the Spanish General Staff to train them to look and march like 11th-century troops, and arrange for them to be housed and fed on location.

People are of two minds about Bronston, and there is little in-between. It's fair to say Bronston was an enigma, but that, of course, is true of many people who have achieved greatness while facing considerable odds. Those who worked for him, actors and technicians, had the highest regard for him. Those who invested in some of the Bronston films vilify him, and use him as an example of the evils of run-away production. To Hollywood, Bronston, who had taken stars and directors away from the U.S. to make profitable films in Spain, was radioactive. There were those who felt the more Bronston succeeded, the more others would emulate his methods. Bronston was a threat to the way things had always been done.

For Spain, where his epic films were largely produced, Bronston was a godsend. He brought large scale filmmaking to the country, and trained a generation of artisans, photographers, lighting technicians and make-up experts.

He gave Spain, struggling with its own place in the world, something to be proud of, for Bronston truly wanted to bring Hollywood to Spain, and for a few brief years, he did just that.

Derek Elley, writing about Bronston in *The Epic Film*, says there really are two names that come to mind when talking about epics, Cecil B. DeMille and Samuel Bronston. Clearly, Bronston was a giant, although a lesser-known giant. The differences between DeMille and Bronston were many, and often laced with irony. DeMille made splashy, sometimes vulgar films. As a Hollywood producer and director, he was among those who helped flush the

Communists out during the McCarthy era. He made one of the first epics, a silent version of *King of Kings* in 1927. In his career as producer and director, DeMille challenged the Hollywood production codes, sometimes choosing to make religious pictures so he could justify themes of violence and sexual decadence.

Thirty-three years later, Bronston remade *King of Kings* in color and widescreen. Ironically, Bronston did not press the production code as DeMille did, but rather emphasized tasteful, restrained historical dramas. Rather than fight or defend the Communists, Bronston left America and made the majority of his films under the repressive Franco Regime. Adding further irony, Bronston hired blacklisted Hollywood writers, some of the same people DeMille was busy running out of town.

Bronston - The Beginnings

Much of Bronston's life is cloaked in controversy and some mystery. His earliest years are not well documented, and family and friends' memories fade or are lost to the passage of time. Bronston himself was not averse to embellishing his early life and there are few alive to argue about it today.

In fact, Bronston kept many details of his early life to himself, and even his family find many of the stories about their father's early years apocryphal.

He was born in Bessarabia (now called the Republic of Moldova) and was one of nine children. There were five brothers, with Samuel being the third, and four sisters.

Samuel's dad was related to one of the chief architects of the Communist philosophy, Leon Trotsky. (Trotsky's real name was Lev Davidovich Bronstein, and Samuel dropped Bronstein for Bronston when he left Russia.) Bronston's father was a baker, an ice cream and desert maker.

Sam's father was not enamored with the Russian revolution, and a plan was formulated to move the children out of Russia one by one, to stay with family in Paris. The boys went first, and the younger girls were exported later.

The family was accomplished musically. The eldest brother, Eli, was a pianist, and later played music at the nickelodeon, perhaps the first exposure of the family to the film business. The second oldest, Richard, also played piano, as did the 4th born son, Jack. Sam played flute, and later became a street hustler, selling ties to anyone who would buy one. He fell in love with photography, taking and selling pictures. Sam claimed he attended the Sorbonne in Paris, having studied history and the arts; the story is even contained in studio publicity, but it is not thought to be true by the family. He also claimed to be flautist with the Paris Symphony, but that is likely also a dubious story.

Bill Bronston says his dad had great command of languages, but was not really highly educated. "Dad spoke very fluent French, very good English, but his heart was in speaking Russian. He could understand almost any language you spoke to him, but couldn't write or spell very well, and was very self-conscious about that. He never really did well or completed school, even though he maintained the façade. There was nobody there to contradict that he did not, as he often claimed, have a Sorbonne education. He was very intimidated about writing letters to us in those days, because he was ashamed of his spelling, in English."

At some point while he was working in Paris, in Sam's mid-20s, he wrote a bad check, and Sam had to flee to the Netherlands with his wife Sarah to avoid a jail sentence. After a short time there, the family moved to England, with hopes of eventually coming to America.

Even in those early days, traits that later define Sam were visible. One was a tremendous amount of energy, often used in the hustling of people and money, with little thought for the consequence. He also didn't develop the skills for handling or managing cash responsibly.

Sam was always looking for money, someone to bankroll him, and when he met his future first wife Sarah, he found someone well off financially, and received help from his future father-in-law.

His photography led him to an interest in film, and although the details aren't clear, somehow he hooked up with an American movie distribution company in Paris. He worked for MGM originally, and later for United Artists.

Hollywood

At age 28 or 29 Samuel Bronston came to America. According to his son Bill, "In 1937, when he arrived by boat, he first wound up in this little tiny boxy apartment in the Bronx, where my aunt's family the Patlach's, lived. There was hardly any room in the apartment, with my mother, living with my aunt, her husband, and her two children, Leon and Jeanette. Jeanette is still alive, by the way, and lives in the Bronx with her 96- or 97-year-old husband. That lasted for a month or two, and all of a sudden my dad went to Washington, D.C. and he somehow hooked up with James Roosevelt, the son of FDR, and some Congressmen and the first thing that happened was he suddenly had some money to go to Los Angeles where he could be near the industry that totally absorbed him.

"The family was absolutely, flabbergasted at how that magic happened. My cousin [Leon Patlach] was always totally amazed that my father could get cheese out of a rock; my father could get resources where no resources existed. He was a divining rod for money. It was amazing. He would raise money not around a project but just borrow money on his own recognizance for his own unspecified vision, and people would give him money. He was in the right place, living in Los Angeles ...”

Los Angeles, the center of the world's movie industry, made sense, with Sam already having contacts after working for those American studios while he was in Europe.

Born Jewish, and with the family name of Bronstein, Samuel began to bury that part of his life, and ostensibly, over the years, worked at convincing himself and others that he was a Catholic, which was reinforced by his subsequent relationship with the Vatican and the Papacy.

His son Bill, who finds his dad was extraordinarily complicated, talked about what drove him. “My father was the most attractive, the most charming man you can imagine. He was just absolutely electric and was very, very elegant and physically reserved. He wasn't a bombastic kind of a guy, but he had an energy. He was the most sophisticated, suave man I have ever seen or met in my life.

“Beyond the façade of aristocratic behavior was this immense fire. He had this dream. He had this conviction about his destiny. And he would always talk about himself in the third person. Bronston's going to do this; Bronston's going to do that. He was so totally egotistical and very, very dynamically defensive about where the soft parts were in his psyche. He was this guy who didn't have a country. Didn't have a language. Didn't have any money and didn't have an education.”

“He was a diminutive guy,” Bronston went on. “He was a Jewish immigrant. So he had very much some of that consciousness, and he was Jewish on top of that. His relatives were a terrifying threat, foremost of course was his association with Leon Davidovitch Bronstein [Trotsky]. He did not live in a time or a community that would have rewarded his relationship with Trotsky or the Russian Revolution. Of course, you don't want to be related to Trotsky and the Russian Revolution, so when he came to the United States he changed his name from Bronstein to Bronston. Over the course of his life, he did everything he could to submerge his Jewish-ness, in every way."

He took a job at Columbia Pictures, and worked on producer Budd Schulberg's *The Adventures of Martin Eden*, based on a Jack London semi-autobiographical novel and starring Glenn Ford and Claire Trevor. It was directed by Sidney Salkow.

From there, Bronston worked on *City Without Men*, another Salkow-directed movie with Budd Schulberg producing, and Bronston listed as executive producer. It starred Linda Darnell and Edgar Buchanan. It was a story about women living in a tight-knit community near the prison where their husbands served time. Darnell's husband was wrongfully imprisoned, and helps her husband escape. The rest of the film involves lawyer Edgar Buchanan trying to make everything right again.

His next film, perhaps growing out of *Martin Eden*, was *Jack London*. Made at United Artists in 1943, Bronston produced this film which starred Michael O'Shea and Susan Hayward. It flowed from a deal Bronston had made with London's widow for the rights to London's books.

A move to 20th Century-Fox gave Bronston producing work on *And Then There Were None*, an Agatha Christie story with Barry Fitzgerald, Walter Huston, and Louis Hayward. Then he was involved on *A Walk in the Sun*, a terrific and well-remembered war picture directed by Lewis Milestone, and starring Dana Andrews, Richard Conte, Lloyd Bridges and John Ireland. The film, still considered a classic, iconic war story, tells the story of an American Platoon during World War II in Italy that comes across a farmhouse occupied by Germans. Some critics feel it is one of the great war films.

Bill Bronston sees a thread in all his dad's early films. "There's no question that there was a genuineness and an integrity to the thrust of his movies. *Jack London, Martin Eden, City Without Men*, all those movies are immensely interesting, character studies about interesting people, heroic people. *A Walk in the Sun* is absolutely incredible. The writer – Robert Rossen, I think, got the screen credit for it but my dad produced that movie and there is documentary evidence of his work. The credit actually is his regardless of what it says on the movie [Lewis Milestone, the film's director is listed as the producer], and the same thing with *And Then There Were None*. [Again, director Rene Clair is listed as producer along with Harry Popkin.] Louie Hayward was a very close friend of ours, he was always in the house, and I was a little kid, around the time I was 4,5,6,7 years old, and all these tremendous people were there all the time. I vividly remember seeking refuge from our house that was constantly filled with actors and directors and the Hollywood coterie that were there all the time. Those films are really compelling. They're really amazing movies. They were deeply gripping and romantic, never big budget. But they have a feel to them which may or may not be due to him. At some level he was the boss, he made all the hiring and story decisions. There's no question about that."

At this point in Bronston's career, information is sketchy and contradictory. Some writers believe Bronston may have had a near nervous breakdown as *A Walk in the Sun* was being prepared. There clearly were financial issues. *Variety* reported in August of 1946 that Bronston had been forced out by creditors who were nervous when the film went over budget. Worse, production began before all the money was in place, a pattern that would be seen later in other Bronston films. Bronston wound up with no money and distribution moved from United Artists to 20th Century-Fox.

Bill Bronston was very young at the time, but said his father was in full control of his faculties. "Dad was working on both *A Walk in the*

Sun and the Agatha Christie *10 Little Indians - And Then There Were None* at the same time. I don't know what was happening at Paramount and with Budd Schulberg's .... Schulberg was my dad's patron and my cousin Leon [Patlach] indicated he was solely responsible for Dad's tenure at the studio producing these projects. Something imploded, one or the other movie, in mid-development, seemed to crash and Dad had 'a nervous breakdown,' which the studio used to explain his being overwhelmed and losing control of the projects. I believe that this was the rationale to cover the business collapse and his withdrawal or being ousted from the projects. As you can see the credited producer of *A Walk in the Sun* is not Dad, although technically and operationally he produced the show. It is a typical signature show with the panoply of young new actors that was his style in that period. My father was not and has never been clinically out of touch but could very well have had a major bout of situational depression that knocked him out. I presume he was down for the count for some months but there was no hiatus of his being away from home ever or his appearing disabled at the dinner table ever."

Whatever happened, these last films ended Bronston's involvement in Hollywood, and his name does not appear on the credits for *A Walk in the Sun* or *And Then There Were None*. It also showed the beginning of a pattern that would reemerge: Excellent films, rife with budget problems. It was said by more than a few in Hollywood that Bronston could make great films, but did not have the skill to manage the prodigious amounts of cash that flowed all around and through his projects.

By the same token, Bronston had no love for Hollywood. He told *Variety* in 1964 that making films there involved "too many tears and not enough action." He went on to suggest that if the Hollywood crowd spent less time complaining and more time making films they would get more done.

He must have been bitter about his experience in Hollywood, but still wanted to make movies. Bronston next appeared at the Vatican, where, in a complex deal involving the Knights of Columbus and the business arm of the Roman Catholic Church, Bronston was contracted for 26 documentaries showing the art treasures owned by the Vatican. Bob Considine narrated the films. Bronston was also involved in a lengthy project to document the Church treasures in an extensive collection of 35mm slides. His contacts with the Vatican during that time proved invaluable when *King of Kings* came along years later, and Bronston somehow and rather miraculously got script approval from the Pope.

The Empire Takes Shape - Spain

Already in Europe, Bronston was clearly eager to produce films where it was less expensive to do so. Many American studios already had production facilities in England and Rome. There were business reasons to do so, and some inviting tax benefits.

Bronston settled on Spain, where studio facilities were available and inexpensive, and labor was bargain-priced. The fact that Spain was run by a dictator, Generalissimo Francisco Franco, was not a deterrent for Bronston.

While many film companies had used Spain for a location, Spain had never been a place for film companies to locate full studios and production facilities. Bronston changed that with *John Paul Jones*, a patriotic sea epic starring Robert Stack and directed by John Farrow (*The Sea Chase, Back from Eternity*). If Bronston saw the irony of creating this flag-waving film in the midst of fascist Spain, those thoughts are lost to us. It was an audacious gamble, but these early moves in Spain helped Bronston create a fully functioning studio with a back lot, office and editing facilities, and storage for props and costumes.

Andrew Marton, a second unit director who did the heavy lifting directing the chariot race in *Ben-Hur*, also worked with Bronston *on 55 Days at Peking* and *The Fall of the Roman Empire*. Marton gives Bronston all the credit for turning Spain into a major center for film production.

"This American financed film industry in Spain has one, and only one person as its originator. Only one person believed in it, built the studio and spent the money to make big pictures in Spain … Samuel Bronston was a really great producer. This man was responsible for, just to name a few, *El Cid, The Fall of the Roman Empire*, and *55 Days at Peking*, all of which were made by a person who cared, who wanted to make important, big, elegant and sumptuous motion pictures, and who didn't skimp. He was like Zanuck, the kind of person who doesn't want to turn the studio into a supermarket, although you can make money that way too. Someone who takes money out of his pocket and puts it into production because he wants to make money by making better pictures." [Interview with Marton by Joanne D'Antonio in the *Directors Guild of America Oral History Project.*]

John Paul Jones was meant to be a patriotic film and was done at the urging of retired Admiral Chester Nimitz, who had become a close friend of Bronston's.

John Paul Jones was designed as a big movie. Budgeted at four million dollars, much of it was shot in Denia on the eastern coast of Spain and other European locations. Starring Robert Stack, with a cameo by Bette Davis, the film only made one million dollars in North America, probably because the script and direction were weak (script by Jesse Lasky and an uncredited Ben Hecht, directed by John Farrow). The film had a lot of flawed history in it, miscasting of television star Robert Stack in the lead, a shortage of adventure and lots of talk. Customers stayed away by the boatload. On the other hand, Bronston was showing that he could put together a first-rate cast with superb production values. It was a talent he would demonstrate over and over again.

Distribution rights were sold to Warner Brothers before production began. Other money came from private investors. Years later, in 1964, after the film flopped, Bronston bought the print and distribution rights from Warner Brothers and tried re-releasing the film on his own. It did no better.

Probably the most significant thing about the film is that it began the methodology that Bronston used to finance his "big" pictures. He wanted the films seen all over the world, so he met with potential distributors in one country after another to get them interested and secure financing. It was a very different model than Hollywood used, where each studio had offices in all the major world markets, and then distributed their own films. It also marked something else unique in Bronston's operations.

He eagerly invited the distributors to be on the sets so they would feel like they were part of the production. He also began shooting his big scenes first, naval battles in *John Paul Jones*, the Temple slaughter in *King of Kings*, Commodus' entry into Rome for *Fall of the Roman Empire* and other such scenes, so as to make those events a form of marketing and fundraising. As a result, the Bronston sets were seldom closed; they were filled with investors Bronston was out to impress. Often Bronston sets were complete buildings, not just false fronts. This kind of construction was not needed for the filming, but I think Bronston loved to have investors, distributors and the press marvel at the depth and breadth of these sets. There had been no other sets ever built like the Bronston sets, and sets like these would never be built again.

At the time of the original release of *John Paul Jones*, Bronston was renting studio space, but he dreamed of true international productions being made in his version of Hollywood operating out of Madrid.

King of Kings was the next Bronston Production. MGM snapped up the distribution rights after the film production was well under way, likely out of fear that it would siphon off audience from *Ben-Hur* which was still in theaters. *King of Kings* advertisements used a similar style of artwork to *Ben-Hur*, the title appearing as if it was cut out of stone.

King if Kings was originally to be directed by John Farrow again, but Nicholas Ray got the job, and brought along Philip Yordan for the screenplay. Yordan stayed with the Bronston organization and became a major source of ideas, as well as a broker for finding blacklisted screenwriters who were willing and eager to work in Europe. Yordan routinely got script credits on the Bronston films, although except for *King of Kings*, Yordan simply procured writers for the films. It wasn't until recent years that the Writers Guild straightened out the credits for the Bronston films, giving writers like Bernard Gordon and Ben Barzman the credit they deserved.

Yordan was a major player in the Bronston organization. An Oscar winner for *Broken Lance* (1954), he became known as a script "fixer" in Hollywood, taking troubled projects on and improving the writing. His knowledge of how Hollywood worked and his contacts with agents helped Bronston in negotiating with big name actors and directors.

King of Kings also solidified Bronston's unique methods of financing these epics.

Bronston's son Bill wasn't fully aware of all the details of how it worked, but he could see the outlines. "It was as elegant as anything that had been created in the world at that time in this business. It was a revolutionized strategy for financing films. One of the problems that he had, and the way in which he got the thing to work was, first of all, Spain had a policy with the United States that blocked currency, which meant that if you made an investment in Spain you could not get your dollars out. You could only get Spanish pesetas out. So the way in which they figured out how to repay the investments was through the creation of a product that they would then sell, that is to say, the film.

"So, if an investor made an investment in Spain they couldn't get their money out of Spain, my dad couldn't pay them out of his treasury, but the revenues of the film would pay back the investor. So it bypassed this very, very significant barrier in currency movement in and out of Spain. That was one of the strategies of getting very significant investment because he could cut a very big deal, sell a piece of a film, and have somebody put money into Spain in order to cover costs, that would then be able to be recouped by the investor, which heretofore had not happened.

"When he found that there was the blocked currency situation he had to have realized that he had to skin that cat to be able to get the necessary out-of-country investment in and to be able to repay the investors, to get around the blocked currency issue. So that was one very fundamental piece of the economic picture, was how to get big money into Spain when the people who put the big money in couldn't get their money out directly. They had to get it out indirectly through the marketing of the film. Second thing had to do with commodities. So part of that was an official dispensation by the Spanish government of a crude oil importation license to my dad's company."

Bernard Gordon, who wrote two films for Bronston, could also see these deals going down from Madrid where he was laboring over scripts for *55 Days at Peking* and *Circus World*. "He [Bronston] would put four or five countries together in terms of moving oil into Spain and putting trucks and other machines out,"

Gordon told me. "But they had iron in Spain. Well, anyway, the whole point in Spain was that they desperately needed oil and other things that they had no hard currency to get. By being able to export what they had, like trucks and railroad cars and things like that, going to Russia and Yugoslavia and Egypt, getting barter. He'd get cotton from Egypt, he'd get pork from Yugoslavia, he'd get oil from Russia, and each of those countries would get what they needed. And it was a really clever ... I don't think he invented it as other people have done and so on, but he made a good deal out of that.

"He was highly regarded in Spain because he was very helpful to their economy. The real trick, of course, was after the film was made the Spaniards didn't really get very much out of it – the foreign money came to Bronston – but Bronston wasn't really interested in making a lot of money. He was interested in becoming the next Cecil B. DeMille. He had a lot of, well, I remember driving through the south of France when they had one of the annual affairs at Cannes, and every big billboard had a Bronston picture up there. Whether it was made, or hadn't been made or would be made or wouldn't be made, there he was, spreading through the whole world. Bronston, Bronston, Bronston pictures. And I thought it was rather ridiculous but maybe it made a point, I don't know."

After *John Paul Jones*, Bronston got into a regular schedule of producing epic films very quickly, something that had never been done before. And from film to film, budgets grew rapidly. *John Paul Jones* was made for four million. In five short years Bronston produced *The Fall of the Roman Empire* for 28 million. What was amazing was how short the production schedules were: Six epic films in six years. Previous mega-films, like *Ben-Hur, Quo Vadis?* or *Cleopatra*, were years in the making. *El Cid*, Bronston's most successful film, began production at the end of November in 1960 and had its first U.S. release in October 1961. It was a staggeringly short time for a film so involved and complex.

In fact, consider the U.S. release dates of all the Bronston Spanish-made films:

John Paul Jones	June 16, 1959
King of Kings	October 11, 1961
El Cid	December 17, 1961
55 Days at Peking	May 28, 1963
The Fall of the Roman Empire	March 26, 1964
Circus World	June 25, 1964

With *El Cid*, Bronston was deepening his ties to Spain as a country. Of course, the subject matter was pure Spanish history, and he got the attention of the Spanish media. He set up a local production company, Samuel Bronston Espanola, which allowed Spanish investment in his films. Bronston had whole villages in his employ making costumes, and foundries making swords and helmets. Spanish builders created his massive sets, and Bronston was bringing in distributors to see all the action.

Tadeo Villalba, one of Bronston's production managers, explained how involved one village became. "One pueblo, Al Molar, which had already supplied manpower for *Alexander the Great* (1955), virtually came to depend on foreign film productions in Madrid for its livelihood. It was a very poor pueblo, and the villagers took a real fancy to working in films. Anywhere a film was being shot in the province, they'd turn up to offer their help. They thought of themselves as film people, and some even came to have important jobs in production. El Molar was about 40 miles from Las Matas [Bronston studios], and the villagers traveled back and forth to get the work done, usually about 12 to 14 hours of work a day, of which 10 hours was for actual filming." [Quoted in *Behind the Spanish Lens.*]

Bronston's dream, later realized, was to recreate Hollywood in Spain on his own terms. Films would be created, sets built, production executed, and even film processing and editing would eventually take place all in Spain.

With *El Cid*, pre-production and production were all in Spain, with post-production in England and the United States. After *El Cid*, Bronston's operation grew, and everything was in Spain. Bronston was self sufficient in terms of production, and had perfected his method of selling his pictures territory by territory.

A major breakthrough for Bronston was his business deal with the DuPont firm, giving him financial guarantees. It enabled Bronston to make bigger and bigger films, but when the DuPont money was yanked, Bronston was headed for bankruptcy and years of legal entanglements.

Bronston's second wife and widow, Dorothea, now living in London, told me she remembered the first meeting with Pierre DuPont III. "Yes, Pierre DuPont invited us to his house in Baltimore. We had lunch with him. He was a dyed-in-the wool Republican so Sam was telling me 'don't tell him that we're Democrats.'"

Bill Bronston explained to me how it all got going. "There was a very significant component of this which had to do with DuPont's underwriting. DuPont had pledged to my dad – probably in *King of Kings* - a million-dollar loan guarantee. My dad actually possessed a check, which Leon controlled. They could walk into any bank and float a loan with that signed DuPont millions, guaranteed. It was not monitored."

The question, of course, is why did the DuPont's agree to a financial arrangement with little or no controls? Bill Bronston explained, "To start with, DuPont wasn't stupid. This was Francis

DuPont, the chairman of the board. It's possible that DuPont initially became involved seeking a tax write-off, on the contention
that *John Paul Jones* was such a bad film – sort of like the plot of the
The Producers – that left to his own devices my dad would lose a
lot of money, which DuPont could write off. And it quickly turned
around with the second film. They began to get that this was an
A+ machine, that they could crank a commercial product. I think
DuPont was enamored by my dad's pitch, and the creativity of his
production strategy.

"Leon told me that my dad never met again with DuPont after
the first time or two and avoided him assiduously, for whatever
reason. My cousin was the bagman and was *the* DuPont contact.
Any business that had to be carried out with DuPont, Leon carried out. Leon took the guarantee from bank to bank, to piece
together the funding that they needed. And the problem was that
they, without prior approval, used the guarantee over and over to
pile up debts beyond the guarantee and when the business came
down there was a major deficit in the area of $15-$25 million that
DuPont was stuck with. It was that compounding of the loans in
order to finance this rolling production. Because what happened
was that each production would go over budget. He had to borrow money from the next project to fulfill the first project, so the
next project was in the hole to begin with and then it would go
over budget.

"The million-dollar guarantee was not a one-to-one loan. It
was a guarantee against a larger loan - they didn't borrow a million against a million. The guarantees were a leveraging tool, because they had other assets. But the DuPont guarantee became
the trigger for successfully locking in the next loan. So there was
borrowing going on. American borrowing as well as international
borrowing, because one of the things that they were trying to do

was build flexible credit system around the world that would finance, from England, from France, from Italy, because what they
were trying to do was to build up a credible production impact by
virtue of how they constructed the films, both economically and
artistically. One after another, Bronston created a burst of spectacular films of high quality and at breakneck speed.

"Each film had its superstar Italian actors, superstar French
actors, superstar British actors, superstar American actors, which
were the box office draw to the distributors. So the films were created extremely intentionally as international showcase events fea-
turing the biggest box office possibilities that they were able to
capture in any given film for any given market, including Japanese,
Chinese. You have, in every instance, a whole variety of multinational talent in there."

It was a brilliantly conceived organization, but at best it was
a house of cards. When the interest in epic films began to quickly
wane, which it did around the release of *Cleopatra* (1963), the entire Bronston empire began to collapse. Distribution of the films
moved from Allied Artists in the U.S. to Paramount, and money
was more closely watched.

The End

Although *55 Days at Peking* had modest profits, Bronston was
well down the production path of the lavishly expensive *The Fall of
the Roman Empire*. At a cost of 28 million dollars, the film had almost no hope of being a money maker, and even with pre-financ-
ing, *Fall of the Roman Empire* and *Circus World* together were already
24 million dollars in the hole. Both films were completed, but neither one had been released. At this point, DuPont wanted to see a
trustee appointed to watch and control expenditures, and Bronston agreed voluntarily. Of course, stopping the flow of money in

February of 1964 was too late. The extravagance of sets, salaries (a million dollars just for Sophia Loren), and the props and costumes that were all built by hand for thousands of extras were already bought and paid for. Bronston must have seen it coming. For *Circus World*, scheduled to be the next big film, the budget was only eight million dollars. For Samuel Bronston, who once bragged that he would never even touch a film that cost less than 10 million dollars, it was a sobering comedown.

Circus World, even at a smaller budget, was a financial and largely artistic disaster, arising out of another chaotic pre-production process, changing directors, and problems with the script and the ever temperamental John Wayne. Paramount, who had worldwide rights to distribute the film, took a bath. DuPont swore that Bronston would never make another film, and Bronston, trying to be a gentleman to the end, quickly agreed to return the production guarantees.

The fight with DuPont went on for years, leaving the ownership and distribution rights to the films open for question during the protracted battles. Bronston hired famed attorney Louis Nizer, but it only made the inevitable drag on. Soon, Spanish banks that had invested in Bronston's films were suing DuPont for halting the completion guarantees.

Bronston's courtroom battles worried Paramount, which had quite a bit of its own money tied up in the Bronston operation. The government of Spain was also nervous, because Bronston had been a tremendous source of income and prestige.

As pressure increased, Bronston closed his New York offices after laying off half his staff in March of 1964.

While the industry watched and spread rumors about Bronston's fate, he continued to be upbeat, telling the March 18, 1964 issue of *Variety,* "I'm entitled to get short of money like everybody else." The same week, his executive vice president of production, Paul Lazarus Jr., resigned.

Bronston remained optimistic, trying to protect his company and his good name. "For the past 25 years, I have devoted my life to motion picture production and the establishment of a reputation for artistic and business integrity. I assure all who are associated with me in my ventures that all steps will be taken to protect their interests. I also assure exhibitors throughout the world that I will continue to produce pictures for their screens, and I am confident that my two current releases, *The Fall of the Roman Empire* and *Circus World,* will be successful at the box office as advance reports from impartial sources indicate they should be." [Bronston quoted in *Variety* March 23, 1964.]

It was wishful thinking. While critics, as always, praised the production quality of the films, moviegoers showed little interest.

In 1971, fighting the bad publicity wave, Bronston announced new productions, including *Isabella of Spain, Night Runners of Bengal* and *Brave New World*.

For *Isabella of Spain,* it was a Bronston return to Spanish history that had been so profitable with *El Cid.* The film was cast with Glenda Jackson in the title role and John Phillip Law. The problem, and it was a knotty one, was how to present Isabella's character. She was a hero in Spanish history, but too much of the world she was the Queen who drove the Jews out of Spain. How to sell and market the film to a worldwide audience seemed quite a feat, and there was a great deal of carping from Hollywood. Peter Besas, who was *Variety's* Spain correspondent, told me he went to see Bronston at the Madrid Hilton and asked him how he could ever make a movie about Isabella that would please an audience. Besas told me, "Bronston was vague, and glossed over the difficulties," almost as if he believed he could will the film into existence.

Although pre-production started, none of those films was ever made.

With DuPont refusing to underwrite any further Bronston production, and lawsuits being rapidly filed by both sides, things were looking grim. By 1965 the court hearing the cases estimated Bronston had liabilities of 35 million dollars.

There also must have been some glee in Hollywood about Bronston's problems. They hated to see production moving out of the U.S. and they liked seeing big stars go overseas even less. The film industry followed Bronston's legal problems intensely, and some undoubtedly saw his fall as comeuppance for mocking American filmmaking practices and his early successes.

After he left Spain, Bronston headed for Texas. He believed it was a place where financiers were more adventurous and he wanted to get first-rate medical care for his second wife, Dorothea, who was dealing with breast cancer.

"He went there," according to Bill Bronston, "because he thought that in Texas he could find financing. It was still a wild west area and he was looking for very, very easy financing that was not eastern-controlled financing. He knew that he had incurred the undying wrath of DuPont, and that DuPont had bought a legal mercenary to stay on my dad, to block any loan that my dad would ever try and put together with a bank ever again, ever. DuPont swore that my dad would never make another movie or borrow a dollar again, from anybody. He went to Texas to try and escape the chokehold DuPont had on him. He made a bad enemy. And he didn't have to. It's just that my dad never really exerted the control over what he spent out as opposed to what came in, and he always believed that there was an endless potential for money. Always.

"My dad absolutely believed he could make anything happen.

He so trusted his persona and his ability to either bedazzle or emotionally leverage his way through getting resourced. He would so utterly get under people's skin, so beguile them. Women, men, it didn't matter. He would just go after getting fresh blood, and promise anything. And in significant circumstances not be able to pay the money back on time, and just let people go down. He was not a responsible, ethical man, especially when he felt his survival was at stake. I'm his son. But he could deliver. He made a bunch of movies that were the biggest movies in the most unusual and original way of financing that the business had ever seen. He broke away from the constraints of studio control, created an empire in Spain, financed his movie with commodities rather than bank loans, and set up a pre-distribution global sales system that brought money in."

"I don't know whether that was his original idea," continued Bronston, "but he really developed it. He showed that it could be done. He brought in millions of independent dollars to bankroll his films before they were there. He went straight to territorial distributors and promised them a big movie outside of the studio system, and delivered it on time. I'm going to give you *El Cid*. I'm going to give you *The Fall of the Roman Empire* in 18 months, in 14 months, in 12 months it'll be in your hands.

"He had a machine that brought in all these distributors and all these territorial guys that was like the United Nations. They all came to Madrid and they had these parties and these extravaganzas. The printed promotional materials were glorious. The printing work that they did in order to market their film and to show the global network was magnificent. My dad was a globalist in terms of figuring out his dollars and everything, and I think it was partly because he was always, always, always an outsider. He never became part of the Hollywood establishment. He badmouthed them, probably because he couldn't get in, and why he couldn't get in is a very, very interesting story."

Bill Bronston sighed slowly, and added, "One of the mysteries of my dad's psychology and his behavior is his perceived and actual relationship to the business. He was not a company man. He was a little Jewish immigrant from Russia, just like the original cinema moguls. He was a total original. There was nobody like him, except these other guys who were hugely successful in the business, the Mayers and the Goldwyns and the Cohens. He was an original guy."

This is echoed by Dorothea Bronston, Bronston's second wife who now lives in London. "What I found most interesting in him is his way of thinking. He wasn't tied in by other people's clichés of what you ought to do, and that worked both ways for him. I was admiring of him in the way that he went about things, and the way he figured out things. When he went to Europe from the United States he said he thought – we were always short of money - and he thought that he could interest people over there in his ideas, over here."

Bronston was a charming, but complicated man. Always very proper and formal, he was never seen unless he was dressed up and wearing a tie.

Bill Bronston struggled once to get his father casual. "I must tell you my father always dressed immaculately. He didn't pass a day in his life without a tie on and a suit on, until he didn't know what a suit was because of the magnitude of the Alzheimer's. He wore a suit and a tie every day of his life. First thing in the morning he'd get up and put it on. It didn't matter what. I had him here when he was in his 70s already. I was in my late 40s. I was born when he was 31. And I somehow was able to get him to come on vacation with me. He was already injured [from oncoming Alzheimer's] to come on a vacation with me with my girlfriend at the time and my two children. And I had to go to the store to get him a complete wardrobe, because he didn't have anything but suits.

"We were going into Mendocino and Fort Bragg and to the beach area and all he had was suits and ties. He came with suits and ties and I said, 'Pop, you're not even going to see a tie. This is just us relaxing and it's inappropriate to wear a suit and a tie. It's inappropriate. You can look good but you've got to wear casual clothes. And you've got to wear this windbreaker.'

"So I bought him all these clothes, very nice Izod shirts, whatever it was I bought him a couple of outfits. And after that trip they were left at the house. And that was the one and only time in his life that I know of that he was not in a suit and tie. There was a certain discipline and a habituation to his lifestyle and identity that was ironclad."

Making films was Bronston's life, but those close to him, including Dorothea, his wife of 20 years, says the money problems that came with creating his epics was always on his mind.

"I was conscious of Sam being preoccupied, period. That's how he was. And with the money, yes. I can remember one time when he was always worried about the money, and he was always borrowing everywhere. I found it rather difficult but that's how he was. I wasn't sure if he was paying any of it back. I think he was just moving on with it. But I didn't want to get involved with that kind of thing. I can remember one time he told me, he came home and he'd had lunch with Charlton Heston, and Heston was – it was after the film *El Cid* was made – and he was going back to the States, and Sam needed him.

"So they were asking for interviews from him, and he didn't want to stay, Heston, he wanted to go home. And Sam was under such strain and Sam put his face in his hands and cried. And he was very embarrassed about that, he told me when he came home. And I noticed in Heston's book, he was very – what's the word I want? – mournful of a man who cried. And I thought, how ridiculous? I mean, Heston was a Midwestern guy and, you know, walked out shooting with his father, but Sam was a peasant from Bessarabia, Jewish, and was getting in above his head in all of these activities, and a very emotional kind of person. I'd have been surprised if he hadn't cried, to tell you the truth. That's the kind of guy he was. "

Bronston was liked by almost everyone who worked closely with him on the films. The actors, directors, technicians all pretty much thought the world of him. There was, however, little love of some of Bronston's lieutenants, chief among them, Mike Waszynski.

Waszynski was known around the Bronston organization as the "Polish Prince" because he claimed royalty from his native country, and he had airs of royalty about him. He had directed films in Poland through the 1940s, then wound up in the United States as an associate producer on the *Captain Gallant of the Foreign Legion* films with Buster Crabbe, a fifties TV series filmed in Morocco and syndicated in the United States. The producer of the show was Harry Saltzman, who produced several of the James Bond films.

Waszynski was likely a big part of the Bronston financial excesses. His deal, reportedly, was not to get a percentage of the profits, but to get a percentage of the films' budgets. That meant from his standpoint, spending a lot of money was a good thing, and he had no reason to try and keep expenses down.

The late Richard Fleisher, who was asked by Bronston to direct *Nightrunners of Bengal*, was astonished at the waste he was seeing as the film moved into pre-production. Although the film was scuttled when Bronston went bankrupt, he was doing his best to hold costs down while everyone else seemed to want to spend more and more.

"I went about my job of preparing the picture, trying to save money anywhere I could. The resistance from everyone was considerable, even nasty. The art directors, Colasanti and Moore, went into a positive snit when I restrained them from building large portions of sets I knew I would never photograph. The prop-makers sulked when I stopped them from making hundreds of props I didn't need. And so it went, right down the line. Everyone was used to wallowing in unlimited funds. Economy and discipline were anathema." [Fleisher in his autobiography, *Just Tell me When to Cry*.]

Later, Fleisher was surprised to have Waszynski tell him that while his planned budget for the film was fine, he would soon be seeing a new budget that was much higher, and to simply keep quiet about it. It was clear to Fleisher the new budget was there to provide a pad for skimming money off the top.

As projects were announced, and then never materialized, Bronston began to fade into the background.

His name resurfaced again in 1972 during more of the endless hearings related to his bankruptcy. During a deposition to try and determine what assets Bronston had, he entered into this testimony.

> Q. Do you have any bank accounts in Swiss banks, Mr. Bronston?
> A. No, sir.
> Q. Have you ever?
> A. The company had an account there for about six months, in Zurich.
> Q. Have you any nominees who have bank accounts in Swiss banks?
> A. No, sir.
> Q. Have you ever?
> A. No, sir.

It was later determined that Bronston indeed had some of his own money (about $180,000) in a personal Swiss account, so the attorneys for the creditors charged Bronston with perjury. A jury agreed, and so did the Court of Appeals.

The case went all the way to the United States Supreme Court, where Bronston's conviction was reversed. The court held that the questions were not properly framed and that Bronston was telling the truth when he said his company had an account there. He was not specifically asked about his own personal account, and he did not volunteer it.

In a unanimous ruling, the high court found that, while Bronston's answer was "shrewdly calculated to evade," it did not rise to the level of perjury because he told the literal truth. U.S. v. Bronston, which gave rise to the "literal truth" doctrine, remains among the most quoted cases on perjury law.

When former President Clinton was impeached, among the articles of impeachment was a charge that Clinton lied about his relationship with Monica Lewinsky and Paula Jones to the Grand Jury. Lawyers for President Clinton cited the Bronston case in arguing that the President may have been misleading but did not lie.

Walter Phillips Jr. was an Assistant United States Attorney and the man who prosecuted the government case against Bronston. He had been given the case after the original government attorney left the office. He told me he felt the case against Bronston was weak, and not winnable. While he felt that Bronston was trying to mislead the government, the government attorneys did not ask him the right question and Bronston had no reason to answer questions he was not specifically asked.

On the other side of the case was attorney Shelden Elsen, who defended Bronston both in civil cases and in the criminal perjury case. Elsen, who still practices law in New York City, told me Bronston was a charming man, but certainly was wasteful when it came to money. He believed the perjury charges against Bronston carried no weight, and was pleased when the Supreme Court ruled in Bronston's favor.

Elsen has many memories of his work with Bronston; perhaps one of the most poignant was when Bronston suggested Elsen meet him in London. When he arrived, Bronston invited Elsen to see a play, called *The Winslow Boy*. The play was about a young boy who was wrongly accused of stealing when he was at the Naval Academy. His family defended him with their last dollar, and eventually, when all looked hopeless, the boy was found innocent. Elsen told me the invitation to see the play with Bronston was Bronston's way of saying he was innocent of all the charges being leveled against him, and he was hoping for his attorney's trust.

Still, Bronston operated in ways that turned heads. Elsen told me a story of one of Bronston's associates who was always getting blank checks from Bronston that were already signed. Many of these checks were cashed in large amounts, and certainly made the Bronston organization look financially undisciplined. Elsen told me when he asked Bronston about these unsigned checks he said anyone filling in amounts of money simply had no authorization to do so, but the questions remained, of course, as to why Bronston had ever signed blank checks to begin with?

Elsen was instrumental at getting Bronston to declare personal bankruptcy to protect what little money he had left. With that done, Bronston moved to a small apartment in Houston where he still believed he could be a deal maker and create big, important films.

His wife Dorothea told me Sam felt there was a lot of money in Texas, and that her husband could get his hands on it. "Sam always said, 'Those people take chances and have money so I'm to go there, if they can help me out.' He did a lot of borrowing."

As Bronston's age advanced, he continued to work the phones, tried to talk up deals, and tried to get over the moat that Pierre DuPont had dug around his life.

He lived on borrowed money from family, friends, and potential investors. As he had done throughout his life, Bronston could literally charm a wallet out of someone's pocket.

Bronston had his hands in a few films that were produced. When the 1966 Argentinean Western, *Savage Pampas* came out, Bronston, although he was not credited, co-produced with his old colleague Jamie Prades. It starred Robert Taylor and Ron Randall. Randall had a major role as Lucius in Bronston's *King of Kings*. During the same year, Bronston co-produced (uncredited) *Dr. Coppelius*. It was a film based on the Delibes' Ballet "Coppelia.' It starred Walter Slezak and Caludia Corday. In 1984 Bronston's name appeared again on a film as producer, along with Albina du Boisrouvray, this time in an adventure-romance directed by Alan Corneau, *Fort Saganne,* and starred Gerard Depardieu and Phillippe Noiret. It was an expensive film for a French release, costing about six million dollars.

Sheldon Elsen told me he saw Bronston when he came to New York in the late 1970s because Bronston wanted to produce some Broadway shows. Elsen told me Bronston did not seem quite right, and, indeed, it might have been early signs of Alzheimer's Disease.

Bronston fought the onset of Alzheimer's for over a decade and a half, but finally he was beaten down by loss of memory and the often severe pneumonia that frequently afflicts Alzheimer's patients.

He died on January 12, 1994 at a hospital near Bill Bronston's home in Sacramento. His ashes were taken to Madrid, where there was a memorial service in the country that Sam Bronston had thrust into the forefront of film production.

The Assets

The chaotic nature of the Bronston film production, combined with the years of legal wrangling during the bankruptcy, left little in the way of tangible assets. Props, costumes and artworks were sold off in a series of auctions to pay creditors. The Bronston Studio itself was sold and for a few years became the Luis Bunuel Studios, then came to be owned by the Spanish Television Network. In 1984, the former Bronston Studios hosted the filming of *Rustler's Rhapsody*, a comedy western directed by Hugh Wilson (*Police Academy*) and starring Tom Berenger, Patrick Wayne and Andy Griffith. It was quite a ways down for the studio that had hosted the fall of Rome.

The Bronston films, other than *King of Kings* which is owned by Warners, have not, until now, been available on home video in North America. *El Cid*, which was restored by Martin Scorsese more than ten years ago, was under the control of Disney. Paramount owned the *Fall of the Roman Empire* and *Circus World*. *55 Days at Peking* was available on VHS tapes but is now long out of print. There was a laser disc of the film, but that format is dead. There were also copies of the *Fall of The Roman Empire* and *Circus World* on laser distributed by Image Entertainment and Criterion offered the restored *El Cid* on laser. Happily, as I've reported, the Weinstein Company has acquired the DVD rights to these films and is lovingly restoring them and collecting extras for DVD release.

This is tremendous news for those who have been impatiently awaiting true high quality releases on DVD. Now, for the first time in more than 40 years, people will be able to see these Bronston epics as they were meant to be seen, in anamorphic widescreen, with multi channel audio.

Because of the complicated auctions of the films rights, most of the Bronston epics have been available in Europe and Asia, but the print quality is not always pristine and the audio is often muffled or in mono. Collectors in the United States, before the imminent release of the discs here, were forced to import these largely inferior releases and play them on universal, region free DVD players.

Samuel Bronston- The Magnificent Showman

Bronston was a man of dreams, and unlike so many of us, he lived his dreams. He brought to life ancient heroes and lost civilizations. He threatened Hollywood dominance and the Hollywood king-makers, and they resented him for it. They resented the Jew who met with the Pope, received honors in the name of Spain's anti-Semitic Queen Isabella, and was able to forge what had become a successful studio to make films about integrity and freedom deep in the heart of a country run by a dictator. The idea of Bron-ston being successful outside the United States grated on many of them. Taking big stars away from Hollywood to make his epics was even worse.

Seeing Samuel Bronston clearly 40 years after his films were made, and more than ten years after his death, is a difficult task. It's a bit like seeing a lighthouse from a distance. It is mostly dark, but there are occasional flashes of light that illuminate.

Bronston was an immensely complicated man who built his business with a vision that was entirely his own. Not wanting to be entangled with Hollywood and its machinations, Bronston in-vented his own method of financing his films and supporting his dreams. His investors were not Hollywood studios, although several bought distribution rights.

His output of films, as I've mentioned, was by any measure prodigious. He released six major films in six years. Some of those films could easily have taken six years alone to make. Five of those six films were genuine epics, and *Circus World*, while not an epic included large scale scenes of the burning circus, and the sinking of a freighter in the harbor at Barcelona. For that scene alone, 600 extras and weeks of preparation were required. *El Cid* or *The Fall of the Roman Empire*, in another producer's hands, could easily have taken three years to create. Such was the magnitude of Bronston's accomplishment.

A man of such deeds is never simple or easy to characterize. He was driven to make great films, about immense deeds, whether it be the founding or destruction of nations (*El Cid, The Fall of the Roman Empire*) or the founding of one of the great world religions (*King of Kings*).

Of the six epics he made in Spain one was a fairly weak biography (*John Paul Jones*) and *Circus World* was created as the Bronston empire was sliding toward oblivion. It was a film without the larger-than-life epic themes Bronston had been creating, but it did have elements that were at least epic in aspiration. That leaves four really impressive films (*King of Kings, El Cid, 55 Days at Peking* and *The Fall of the Roman Empire*), each of which amounts to an incredible achievement in the art of motion picture making.

In 1988, in accepting an award for *El Cid* from the Valledolid International Film Festival at age 80, he said: "I consider myself a 20th Century Artist whose medium consists of the most complicated elements; armies of talented people, huge financing capital, awesome communications technologies and a collective of creative peers whose brilliance and discipline set a standard of quality that is still a global source of inspiration. Over the years, my companies have worked to produce a sense of national and international pride through epic images of heroism, telling the most passionate of stories of all time: the Bible, Spain's mythology, Rome, Peking, the American Revolution .... A world of entertainment.

"In retrospect, of all the characters in my films, I identify most with Sir Alec Guinness' portrayal of the Emperor Marcus Aurelius in his quest for 'Pax Romana,' for I have always been driven by the same hunger for world peace, world harmony, world friendship.

"Times are changing. I miss the great romance that existed in big filmmaking. I miss the values of family, nobility, personal sacrifice and historical awareness that governed our films' heroes ... matters of importance. I miss seeing the kind of cinematic quality, the art and fineness that drove our work and characterized our films."

Samuel Bronston has left us works of unrivaled beauty and inspiration. What he did, no one had done before or since. He was an original, and like all driven men, he had his share of triumphs and tragedies. When the controversies, the politics, and the shaky financing are forgotten, we are left with films that thrill and stimulate our minds to walk with Jesus, to share the victories of El Cid, to contemplate the end of the Roman Empire and the transformation of the Chinese Dynasty.

That Bronston did these things, against all odds, is reason enough to remember him. The films are testimony to this quiet, small, driven man who started with nothing and created a legacy of beautiful and intense cinematic images that are vividly remembered to this day.

Samuel Bronston loved to make movies. More than 40 years later, we still love to watch them.

Some final thoughts

In researching this book Bill Bronston was kind enough to let me search through a basement box that contained what was left of his dad's papers. It was a medium-sized carton that contained photos, posters, script drafts, letters to people Bronston owed money to, and letters negotiating with agents for securing talent for his movies.

I was struck by how sad it was that a man who lived and cre-ated in such a monumental scale could have his life reduced to the contents of a box in a basement. It saddened me as I sat staring at the remnants of a life lived very large by a man who recreated the Roman Forum, employed thousands of cast members, and brought to life on the screen the distant past with a zeal and dedi-cation that was both rare and a treasure for future generations.

I then realized that, like Bronston, most of us will also be re-duced to some papers in a box held in a basement or sitting on a shelf, but few of us will leave an artistic legacy like the one left by Samuel Bronston. His visions of noble deeds and heroic men and women still speak to us almost half a century after they were conceived.

The Epic Films of Samuel Bronston

John Paul Jones (1959)

Cast

John Paul Jones	Robert Stack
Catherine the Great	Bette Davis
Aimee de Tellison	Marisa Pavan
Benjamin Franklin	Charles Coburn
Patrick Henry	Macdonald Carey
King Louis XVI	Jean-Pierre Aumont
John Wilkes	David Farrar
Captain Pearson	Peter Cushing
Marie Antoinette	Susana Canales
Russian Chamberlain	Georges Riviere
Peter Wooley	Tom Brannum
Gunner Lowrie	Bruce Cabot

Production Credits

Produced by	Samuel Bronston
Directed by	John Farrow
Screenplay by	John Farrow, Jesse Lasky Jr., Ben Hecht

Music by	Max Steiner
Cinematography	Michel Kelber
Film Editing	Eda Warren
Art Direction	Franz Bachelin
Set Decoration	Dario Simoni
Assistant Set Decorator	Jose Maria Alarcon
Costumes	Phyllis Dalton
Assistant Director (2nd Unit)	Frank Losee
Sound Effects	Winston Ryder
Special Effects	Roscoe Cline
Technical Advisors	J.L Pratt,
	Captain Alan Villiers

Photographed in 35mm Technirama®

King of Kings (1961)

Cast

Jesus Christ	Jeffrey Hunter
Mary, Mother of Jesus	Siobhan McKenna
Pontius Pilate	Hurd Hatfield
Lucius, the Centurion	Ron Randall
Claudia	Viveca Lindfors
Herodias	Rita Gam
Mary Magdalene	Carmen Sevilla
Salome	Brigid Bazlen
Barabbas	Harry Guardino
Judas	Rip Torn
Herod Antipas	Frank Thring
Caiaphas	Guy Rolfe

Nicodemus	Maurice Marsac
Herod	Gregoire Aslan
Peter	Royal Dano
And as John the Baptist	Robert Ryan

Production Credits

Produced by	Samuel Bronston
Associate Producers	Alan Brown, Jaime Prades
Directed by	Nicholas Ray
Screenplay by`	Philip Yordan
Music by	Miklos Rozsa
Directors of Photography	Franz Planer A.S. C. and
	Milton Krasner A.S.C.
	Manuel Berenguer
Sets and Costume Design	Georges Wakhevitch
Set Decoration	Enrique Alarcon
Sp. Photographic Effects	Lee LeBlanc
General Production Mgr.	Stanley Goldsmith
Supervising Technician	Carl Gibson
Special Effects	Alex C. Weldon
Film Editor	Harold Kress A.C.E.
Murals by	Maciek Piortrowski
2nd Unit Directors	Noel Howard,
	Sumner Williams
Assistant Directors	Carlo Lastricati,
	Jose Maria Ochoa,
	Jose Lopez Rodero
Make-Up	Mario Van Riel,
	Charles Parker
Recording Supervisor	Franklin Milton
Sound Recordist	Basil Fenton Smith

Supervisor of Costuming	Eric Seelig
Hair Styles	Anna Cristofani
Choreography for Salome's Dance	Betty Utey

Photographed in 70mm Super Technirama® and Technicolor®

Filmed at Chamartin Studios -Madrid

El Cid (1961)

Cast

El Cid	Charlton Heston
Chimene	Sophia Loren
Count Ordonez	Raf Vallone
Princess Urraca	Genevieve Page
Prince Alfonso	John Fraser
Prince Sancho	Gary Raymond
Arias	Hurd Hatfield
Fanez	Massimo Serato
Ben Yussuf	Herbert Lom
Al Kadir	Frank Thring
Moutamin	Douglas Wilmer
Don Diego	Michael Hordern
Count Gormaz	Andrew Cruickshank
Don Pedro	Tullio Carminati
Don Martin	Christopher Rhodes
King Ramirez	Gerard Tichy
Bermudez	Carlo Giustini

Production Credits

Produced by	Samuel Bronston
Directed by	Anthony Mann
Associate Producers	Michael Waszynski and Jaime Prades
Screenplay by	Philip Yordan and Frederick M. Frank
Screenplay by	Ben Barzman (uncredited until 1999)
Music by	Miklos Rozsa
Director of Photography	Robert Krasker
Production & Costume Design	Veniero Colasanti and John Moore
Film Editor	Robert Lawrence
(2nd unit)	Manuel Berenguer
Special Effects	Alex Weldon, Jack Erickson
2nd Unit Director	Yakima Canutt
Production Managers	Leon Chooluck and Guy Luongo
Assistant Directors	Luciano Sacripanti, Jose Maria Ochoa, Jose Lopez Rodero
Master of Properties	Stanley Detlie
Supervising Technician	Carl Gibson
Supervising Electrician	Norton Kurland
Sound Recordist	Jack Solomon
Re-Recorded by	Gordon K. McCallum
Sound Editor	Verna Fields
Music Editor	Edna Bullock
Wardrobe Director	Gloria Musetta
Hair Styles by	Grazia De Rossi

Makeup Created by — Mario Van Riel
Murals by — Maciek Piotrowski
Script Supervisor — Pat Miller

Photographed in Super Technirama 70® and Technicolor®
Filmed at the Samuel Bronston Studios- Madrid

55 Days at Peking (1963)

Cast

Major Matt Lewis	Charlton Heston
Baroness Natalie Ivanoff	Ava Gardner
Sir Arthur Robertson	David Niven
Empress Tzu-Hsi	Flora Robson
Sgt. Harry	John Ireland
Father de Bearn	Harry Andrews
Gen. Jung-Lu	Leo Genn
Prince Tuan	Robert Helpmann
Baron Sergei Ivanoff	Kurt Kasznar
Julliard	Philippe Leroy
Dr. Steinfeldt	Paul Lukas
Lady Sarah Robertson	Elizabeth Sellars
Garibaldi	Massimo Serato
Major Bobrinski	Jacques Sernas
Capt. Marshall	Jerome Thor
Smythe	Geoffrey Bayldon
Teresa	Lynne Sue Moon
U.S. Minister	Nicholas Ray

Production Credits

Produced by — Samuel Bronston

Associate Producer	Alan Brown
Executive Associate Producer	Michael Waszynski
Directed by	Nicholas Ray, Guy Green, Andrew Marton
Written by	Ben Barzman, Bernard Gordon, Robert Hamer, Philip Yordan
Original Music by	Dimitri Tiomkin
Director of Photography	Jack Hildyard
Film Editing	Robert Lawrence
Casting	Maude Spector
Production Design	Veniero Colasanti, John Moore
Set Decoration	Veniero Colasanti, John Moore
Costumes	Veniero Colasanti, John Moore
Make Up	Mario Van Riel
Hairdresser	Grazia De Rossi
Production Manager	C.O. Erickson
Second Unit Director	Noel Howard
Master of Properties	Stanley Detlie
Sound Effects Editor	Milton C. Burrow
Music Editor	Richard Harris
Sound Mixer	David Hildyard
Sound Re-Recordist	Gordon K. McCallum
Special Effects	Alex Weldon
Camera Operator 2nd Unit	Manuel Berenguer
Technical Advisor	Col. J.R. Johnson, DSO, OBE, MC

Continuity	Lucie Lichtig
Operations Director 2nd Unit	Andrew Marton

Photographed in Technirama® and Technicolor®
Filmed at the Samuel Bronston Studios - Madrid

The Fall of the Roman Empire (1964)
Cast and Production Crew

Cast

Lucilla	Sophia Loren
Livius	Stephen Boyd
Marcus Aurelius	Alec Guinness
Timonides	James Mason
Commodus	Christopher Plummer
Verulus	Anthony Quayle
Ballomar	John Ireland
Sohamus	Omar Sharif
Cleander	Mel Ferrer
Julianus	Eric Porter
Caecina	Finlay Currie
Polybius	Andrew Keir
Niger	Douglas Wilmer
Victorinus	George Murcell
Virgilianus	Norman Wooland
Cornelius	Michael Gwynn
Marcellus	Virgilio Texera [Teixeira]
Claudius	Peter Damon
Lentulus	Rafael Luis Calvo
Helva	Lena von Martens

Production Credits

Producer	Samuel Bronston
Director	Anthony Mann
Executive Assoc. Producer	Michael Waszynski
Screenplay by	Ben Barzman, Basilio Franchina and Philip Yordan
Music Composed and Conducted by	Dimitri Tiomkin
Production and Costume Design	Veniero Colasanti and John Moore
Consultant	Dr. Will Durant
Film Editor	Robert Lawrence
Photography	Robert Krasker B.S.C.
Associate Producer	Jaime Prades
Second Unit Director	Yakima Canutt
Executive Production Manager	C.O. Erickson
Assistant Director 1st Unit	Jose Lopez Rodero
Assistant Director 2nd Unit	Jose Maria Ochoa
Casting	Maude Spector
Camera Operator	John Harris
2nd Unit Cameraman	Cecilio Paniagua
Title Backgrounds and Murals	Maciek Piotrowski
Sound Mixer	David Hildyard
Sound re-recording	Gordon K. McCallum
Sound Effects Editor	Milton Burrow
Music Editor	George Korngold
Assistant Film Editor	Magdalena Paradell
Special Effects	Alex Weldon
Master of Properties	Stanley Detlie
Supervising Technician	Carl Gibson

Head of Wardrobe	Gloria Musetta
Costumes made by	Ceratelli & Peruzzi, Italy
Make-up	Mario Van Riel
Hairdressing	Grazia De Rossi
Continuity	Elaine Schreyeck
Dialogue Coach	George Tyne

Photographed in Ultra-Panavision® and Technicolor®
Filmed at Samuel Bronston Studios- Madrid

Circus World (1964)

Cast

Matt Masters	John Wayne
Toni Alfredo	Claudia Cardinale
Lili Alfredo	Rita Hayworth
Cap Carson	Lloyd Nolan
Aldo Alfredo	Richard Conte
Steve McCabe	John Smith
Emil Schuman	Henri Dantes
Mrs. Schuman	Wanda Rotha
Giovanna	Katharyna
Flo Hunt	Kay Walsh
Anna	Margaret MacGrath
Molly	Katherine Ellison
Billy Rogers	Miles Malleson
Hilda	Katherine Kath
Bartender	Moustache

Production Credits

Producer	Samuel Bronston

Director — Henry Hathaway
Executive Associate Producer — Michael Waszynski
Music — Dimitri Tiomkin
Screenplay — Ben Hecht,
Julian Halevy [Julian Zimet],
Bernard Gordon and
James Edward Grant

Story by — Philip Yordan and
Nicholas Ray

Production Design — John De Cuir
Costume Design — Renie
Film Editor — Dorothy Spencer
Cinematographer — Jack Hildyard
2nd Unit Cinematographer — Claude Renoir
2nd Unit Director — Richard Talmadge
Assistant Director 1st Unit — Jose Lopez Rodero
Assistant Director 2nd Unit — Terry Yorke
Coordinator of
Circus Operations — Frank Capra, Jr.
Sound — David Hildyard
Dialogue Coach — George Tyne
Executive Production Manager — C.O. Erickson
Special Effects — Alex Weldon
Supervising Technician — Carl Gibson
Supervising Electrician — Bruno Pasqualini
Master of Properties — Stanley Detlie
Casting — Maude Spector
Head of Wardrobe — Anna Maria Feo
Makeup — Mario Van Riel
Hairdressing — Grazia De Rossi
Continuity — Elaine Schreyeck

Continuity 2nd unit   Kay Rawlings

Photographed in Super Technirama-70®
Filmed at Samuel Bronston Studios-Madrid

Hollywood Films of Samuel Bronston (as Producer or Executive Producer)
1942   *The Adventures of Martin Eden*
1943   *City Without Men*
1943   *Jack London*
1945   *And Then There Were None*
1945   *A Walk in the Sun* (uncredited)

Films for the Vatican
1951   *The St. Peter's Excavations* (documentary)
1951   *Mosaics-Pictures for Eternity* (documentary)

Films Bronston Produced after the Closure of his Madrid Studios
1966   *Savage Pampas* (uncredited)
1966   *The Fantastic World of Dr. Coppelius* (uncredited)
1984   *Fort Saganne* (co-producer)

Projects in pre-production but never produced
Brave New World, Captain Kidd, Carmen, Dear and Glorious Physician, Don Quixote, The French Revolution, Isabella of Spain, Magnificent Destiny, Nightrunners of Bengal, Paris 1900, La Belle Epoch, and *Suez.*

Isabella of Spain was quite advanced in production, and Bronston had cast Glenda Jackson and John Phillip Law. Negotiations were underway with Patrick McGoohan when the project collapsed.

For Further Reading

These books were helpful in the preparation of this book and may be of interest to readers for more information about epic films and those who create them.

Andrew, Geoff. *Nicholas Ray* (Charles Letts and Company Ltd., 1991)

Barzman, Norma. *The Red and the Blacklist* (Nation Books, 2003)

Besas, Peter. *Behind the Spanish Lens* (Arden Press, 1985)

Canutt, Yakima. *Stunt Man* (Walker Publishing Company, 1979)

Eisenschitz, Bernard. *Nicholas Ray: An American Journey* (Faber and Faber Ltd. 1993)

Fleischer, Richard. *Just Tell Me When to Cry* - A Memoir (Carroll & Graf Publishers, 1993)

Fletcher, Richard. *The Quest for El Cid* (Oxford University Press, 1989)

Gordon, Bernard. *Hollywood Exile: or How I Learned to Love the Blacklist* (University of Texas Press, 1999)

Heston, Charlton. *In the Arena* (HarperCollins Publishers, 1995)

Koszarski, Richard (ed). *Hollywood Directors 1941-1976* (Oxford University Press, 1977)

D'Antonio, Joanne. *Andrew Marton- A Directors Guild of America Oral History* (The Scarecrow Press, 1991)

Munn, Mike. *The Stories Behind the Scenes of the Great Epic Films* (Illustrated Publications Company, 1982)

Rovin, Jeff. *The Films of Charlton Heston* (Citadel Press, 1980)

Rozsa, Miklos. *Double Life -The Autobiography of Miklos Rozsa* (Hippocrene Books, 1982)

About the Author

Mel Martin has spent most of his professional career as a reporter. He won 2 Emmy Awards and 2 Columbia-DuPont Awards for investigative journalism. He also worked for the BBC in London as a project director for the creation of a news content management system. He then spent 8 years in Seattle working in the new media field, creating solutions for getting news to the web. He now lives in Arizona and is consulting to companies in the broadcast industry. He is an avid amateur astronomer and has published photos of deep sky objects in astronomy magazines and journals.

Index

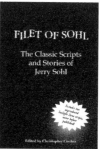

Printed in Great Britain
by Amazon